BRIST & BATH WHODUNNIT?

BRISTOL & BATH WHODUNNIT?

David Kidd-Hewitt

COUNTRYSIDE BOOKS
NEWBURY, BERKSHIRE

First published 2007
© David Kidd-Hewitt, 2007

COUNTRYSIDE BOOKS
3 Catherine Road
Newbury, Berkshire

To view our complete range of books,
please visit us at
www.countrysidebooks.co.uk

ISBN 978 1 84674 052 7

With love to
Jan, Rach, Mike, Paul & Gisela

Designed by Peter Davies
Produced through MRM Associates Ltd., Reading
Typeset by CJWT Solutions, St Helens
Printed by Cambridge University Press

All material for the manufacture of this book
was sourced from sustainable forests.

CONTENTS

FOREWORD

Murder is always around us, always a possibility, and sometimes closer than we care to imagine. Husbands, a wife, a son-in-law, lovers, true friends and casual acquaintances all feature as murderers in this collection of true 20th century murder cases in the Bristol and Bath area. It is wise therefore not to think of this ultimate crime as solely associated with the frenzy of a murderous attack by a stranger, but, of course, these do feature too.

Take 37-year-old Mrs Margaret Backhouse, married for ten years to 43-year-old Graham, with two young children, happy on their farm in the hamlet of Horton until her 'loving' husband decided that money was more important than she was in his life. What happened to Margaret and an innocent neighbour beggars belief but truth is definitely stranger than fiction in what proves to be an explosive murder story.

Love can also prove so powerful that it severs the very special relationship it gave rise to. The First World War story of Private Albert Cross and his dear wife Bessie proved to be an emotional roller-coaster of passion, hate, adultery and murder. And, if you can have such a thing as poignancy and murder side by side, then this Bristol tragedy has it.

A red mist before the eyes – anger – then murder – then disbelief. This is what William Bartlett claimed when he discovered his fatally-beaten wife Marjorie at The Chocolate Box, their Bath sweetshop. This case allows an unusual glimpse behind the scenes in a murder defence trial – the very first one for a new KC, Mr J.D. Casswell, who subsequently features in many murder cases in the Bristol and Bath area.

However, even he was taken aback by the sexual adventures behind the lace curtains of suburban Henleaze. Defending a certain Mrs Ann Cornock, whom he nicknamed 'pokerface', the murder trial turned into something almost as bizarre as the sexual acts that led to her husband Cecil's untimely death. Adultery, cross-dressing, bondage, corporal punishment and bathtime with a difference may lighten the mood but the end result was still murder – or was it? What role did lodger Ken have in all this?

Adulterous relationships also take us to the closed community of woodland folk, scratching a precarious living on their shanty smallholdings in Hanham Woods, just outside Bath, in the 1930s. Coveting thy neighbour's wife led to the additional sin of her murder by a certain Mr Franklin who also wanted her husband equally dead. He enters the record books, not as the murderer, but as the defendant in the shortest murder trial on record – six minutes from entering the dock to receiving the death penalty.

Greed and avarice are common triggers to murder, sometimes hiding under a camouflage of pretence. Reginald Ivor Hinks claimed to be the perfect, caring son-in-law yet devised very special plans for his father-in-law's demise in the leafy suburbs of Bath. His murder technique somehow managed to mix farce with the horror of taking a life. Forcing your elderly father-in-law, stricken with a double hernia and dementia, to endure a ten-mile 'run' is imaginative to say the least.

This is a lesson in how **not** to murder your father-in-law.

We might know 'whodunnit' with these murders but, frighteningly, there are many still unsolved. Avon and Somerset police have an active and successful 'cold cases' team, but they still want your help today. Who murdered young mother Shelley Morgan before dumping her in woods at Backwell? Who launched a savage attack on Helen Fleet in Weston? Who brutally clubbed and stabbed charity-worker Beryl Culverwell at her home in Bath? Someone out there knows something about these cold cases – perhaps it's you?

Lastly we visit *Crimewatch UK* which, since 1984, has proved its worth in tracking down all types of criminals. The case of the bogus gasman of Bedminster is typical and it is clear that *Crimewatch UK*, together with public participation, played a major role in catching the callous murderer.

When you have read this book, do remember the sound advice given out by Nick Ross after every *Crimewatch UK* programme, 'Don't have nightmares, do sleep well.'

David Kidd-Hewitt

ACKNOWLEDGEMENTS

The complexities of researching and writing about true crimes across the 20th century, within a specific geographical area, dictates that we must tap into the knowledge, expertise and goodwill of a range of organisations and individuals. I have been fortunate, as ever, to enjoy facilities of the Aladdin's cave that is the British Newspaper Library at Colindale with their friendly and instructive assistance and, in particular, I'd like to thank Jim Coyle and Victor Bristoll.

I very much appreciated the warm welcome extended to me by the *Western & Somerset Mercury* newspaper in Weston-super-Mare – thank you Sue Harding. Permission to use the newspaper's archived material was of crucial assistance indeed, and gratefully received. Thank you for this to Judi Kifiel (editor) and Clare Hayes (news editor).

Weston-super-Mare Library also made me very welcome and gave me every assistance possible. Thank you to Lesley Flood for organising my visit, and to Sarah Bowen, Nicki Bobbette and Jaquelyn James for putting up with me whilst I was there.

Thanks to Marina Coles who answered my plea in the local paper for old newspaper headlines – your assistance was so helpful and welcoming, as was that of DC Sean Filby, James Makin and Jan Pow. My thanks go to John Morris of the Bath Maternity Society for help with the Beryl Culverwell case; to Philip Jay of Loxton Garage for talking to me about the Noreen O'Conner story; to Terry Forshaw of Amber Books for all his assistance; to Emma Horsfield at Hodder Headline; and to Paul Townsend for access to material on his amazing web-site www.bristolhistory.com.

Finally my grateful thanks to broadcaster and journalist Nick Ross.

1
THE HORTON VENDETTA

'YOU NEXT'

Tucked towards the bottom of page 2 of *The Times* on 10th April 1984 was the following item:

> A farmer's wife, whose family had received threatening telephone calls during the past fortnight, was seriously injured yesterday when a bomb went off as she was starting the family car. Mrs Margaret Backhouse, aged 37, underwent more than 6 hours surgery at the Frenchay Hospital, Bristol while doctors removed metal and debris embedded in her side by the force of the blast.

This bizarre and violent story would soon evolve into headlines about a tragic village murder, as well as a significant text-book entry into the increasingly complex world of forensic science.

The small hamlet of Horton, near Chipping Sodbury, was buzzing with the news of the explosion. Neighbours and villagers wished Maggie Backhouse a speedy recovery from severe injuries to her legs and buttocks. They were also aghast at the news that this appeared to be a deliberate act of murder. Indeed, the detective leading the inquiry, Detective Inspector Tom Evans, was reported in the local media as saying, 'There has been a recent history of anonymous phone calls to the home threatening the husband and the family.'

It was assumed by all that the intended victim was 43-year-old

The wreckage of Graham Backhouse's car.
(Western Media Publishing)

Mr Graham Backhouse, but that morning it was Maggie who set off from their home at Widden Farm to collect supplies from the local vet.

Her husband Graham had lent her his car as her own had suddenly developed a fault. She turned the ignition key, which triggered the bomb that nearly led to her death. She had managed to stagger from the car before collapsing in agony and was then rushed to hospital.

Graham Backhouse was distraught, as he had doubts about how seriously the police had been taking the previous telephone threats to his family. He had made constant calls to them about these threats to his life, and the explosion now proved how deadly serious they really had been, not only to himself, but to his wife and their two young children, Harry aged 10 and Sophie aged 8. They could have all been in that car that morning – it did not bear thinking about.

However, over the preceding weeks Detective Inspector Evans had been taking very seriously Graham Backhouse's claims that he was the victim of a conspiracy to murder. He had told the police of anonymous telephone calls, and showed them some letters clumsily printed in block capitals that threatened his life in no uncertain terms. It was reported that Backhouse admitted to having had a number of affairs with local married women and, as a result, certain people perhaps had reasons to dislike him intensely, but to want to murder him would seem to be excessive. Prior to the car bomb, what had really brought home the great gravity of the threat was an extremely gruesome discovery. On his rounds, a stockman at the farm had discovered the severed head of a sheep carefully impaled on a stake close to the farm house with a note attached. Written in block capitals were the two words:

YOU NEXT

Apart from the prospect of an irate husband wanting revenge on the farmer for seducing his wife, there was, Backhouse claimed, a dispute over land boundaries and rights of way with a neighbour, Colyn Bedale-Taylor, aged 63. It is well known for arguments over land rights to far outweigh any falling-out over sexual indiscretions.

This appeared to the police to be the strongest motive to explain the threats to Backhouse's life. However, Colyn Bedale-Taylor denied any knowledge of such behaviour and there was no evidence against him whatsoever.

With Maggie Backhouse injured in hospital, and not knowing what the next action of the attacker might be, Graham Backhouse and his family were given 24-hour police protection, whilst the investigation continued. The analysis of the home-made bomb, which detectives believed had been planted to kill Graham Backhouse, revealed two sections of metal pipe packed with powder extracted from around a dozen or so shotgun cartridges. Loaded with thousands of lead pellets, the bomb had been carefully positioned to face upwards through the driver's seat. It was a miracle Maggie Backhouse had survived such a deadly booby-trap.

Now revealed as a village vendetta, locals awaited the next

The forensic scientist holds up the threatening letters which Graham Backhouse claimed were sent to him. (Western Media Publishing)

episode in the story with a mixture of curiosity and trepidation. Around nine days had passed since the bombing, and the police were steadily collecting statements and investigating possible motives, whilst carefully watching over the Backhouse family at Widden Farm. On 18th April Detective Inspector David Edwards called to see Graham Backhouse, who told the detective rather ungratefully and curtly that he was fed up with the police guard placed on him for his protection, and wanted to get back to normality. He claimed that whilst his wife was safe in hospital, he'd rather the bomber have another go at him, to bring the culprit out into the open so that he could be caught. As long as the police stood guard this was unlikely to happen. Backhouse said he was installing an alarm system with a panic button linked to the police station, so they should now pack up and go. The police authorities decided to withdraw the police surveillance in line with his wishes.

On the evening of 30th April, the newly-installed alarm

alerted the police to the fact that something was indeed happening at Widden Farm. When they entered the farmhouse, they were confronted by a bloody scene. Police Constable Richard Yeadon said he saw the body of Mr Colyn Bedale-Taylor lying in a passageway, with a hole in his chest. He was clutching a Stanley knife in his right hand.

'I stepped over the body and saw Mr Backhouse lying in a curled-up position in the entrance to the lounge. He was sobbing,' Yeadon later testified. The police constable could see extensive injuries to Backhouse's chest and face. He looked up at Yeadon and repeatedly said, 'I did not kill his son.' Colyn Bedale-Taylor was clearly dead. He had been shot though the chest with a double-barrelled shotgun.

It seemed that the vendetta had reached its climax – Backhouse's mysterious would-be assassin had been slain and Backhouse had survived. He and his family were now safe. But why had Bedale-Taylor attacked him like this? Why was Backhouse repeating, over and over, 'I did not kill his son'?

Graham Backhouse needed careful medical attention to deep cuts to his face and body. In fact, one wound ran from ear to chin, and required 80 stitches. He explained to the police that Bedale-Taylor had called with a craft knife claiming, rather oddly, that he had been asked to come and repair some furniture. Backhouse felt very threatened by this bizarre and unexpected visit and told him there was no furniture to repair. He then claimed that Bedale-Taylor had said that God had sent him, and accused Backhouse of being the cause of his son Digby's death in a car crash eighteen months previously. Bedale-Taylor then confessed that he had been the person who sent the threatening notes, rigged up the sheep's head warning, and made and planted the bomb in Backhouse's car. Bedale-Taylor then lunged at him with the scalpel-sharp craft knife. Backhouse had run inside, grabbed his gun and warned Bedale-Taylor to leave. He refused and continued his frenzied attack on Backhouse accusing him of killing Digby. Backhouse had then shot Bedale-Taylor in self-defence. He told the police, 'I ran into the hallway and grabbed a gun; Bedale-Taylor was still after me. I shouted I had got a gun but he still kept coming and I shot him. He fell back and I shot him again and that was it.' He added, 'I was very frightened.'

It all seemed to fit the scene witnessed by the officers that night. Was this case now closed?

One very important feature, though, presented a puzzle for the detectives. Geoffrey Robinson, a forensic expert from the Home Office Forensic Laboratory at Chepstow in Gwent, had been to the crime scene. He had made a painstaking investigation of the evidence left behind after the alleged struggle with Colyn Bedale-Taylor, a man possessed with anger according to Backhouse, clutching a craft knife and lunging at his victim to slash and kill. Then there was Backhouse himself, taken aback by such an attack, running to grab his gun and first warning and then shooting Bedale-Taylor to end the knife attack on his face and body.

The puzzle was that the physical and forensic scene told a different story altogether. What had really happened that evening was as vivid to Robinson as if he'd been there, and the key to his understanding lay in examining the many drops of blood at the scene. During fights, particularly if you are attacked with a knife, in defending your face, blood will spurt and drop and splash in all sorts of ways that reflect the intensity and direction of the fight, or the desperation of the fleeing, turning, twisting victim to prevent death or serious injury. In the work of forensic scientists, blood is seen to drip, spray, ooze, smear and get flung – so blood pattern analysis gives a unique view of something that was not witnessed yet leaves a picture almost as clear as if it had been.

Moreover, furniture will fall over and be damaged in a genuine fight and its relationship to the sequence of events will show if a chair fell onto the blood or the blood onto the chair, or gun butt, or knife handle, or whatever was used – it depicts movement very clearly. The puzzle for Geoffrey Robinson was that the blood droplets showed a victim who seemed to have stood still whilst being cut with a knife, rather than fighting off his attacker. Blood flung from a fight such as Backhouse described would appear in exclamation mark shapes everywhere, whereas the blood evidence in the room was in the form of

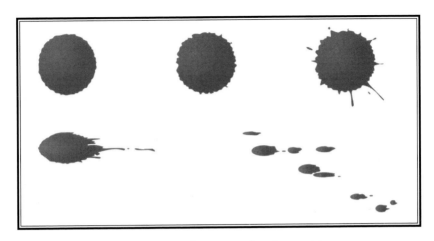

Blood spatter analysis provides clear evidence.

circular drops, allowed to fall from someone standing still. Kitchen chairs had been knocked over onto the perfectly formed droplets with 'crenated' or toothed edges. There was no blood splashed onto the chairs, except a long smear left on a chair back by Backhouse's hand. Yet, despite this evidence of a bleeding hand, no blood at all was found on the gun he grabbed in desperation, to shoot his attacker.

Geoffrey Robinson's suspicions were confirmed by the position of Colyn Bedale-Taylor's body in the passageway from the front door to the kitchen. There were no blood droplets along the passage to link with those in the kitchen. The forensic picture therefore was of Backhouse shooting Bedale-Taylor at point-blank range with no suggestion of any attack to support a claim of self-defence. He then inflicted the craft-knife wounds upon himself whilst in the kitchen, standing still and steeling himself against the intense pain as he cut deeply into his own face and body, the blood dropping into tell-tale perfectly formed circles rather than the splashes, smears and exclamation marks of a genuine victim fleeing and fighting. Backhouse then toppled chairs to give the impression that a fight had taken place.

Dr Kennard, a pathologist, explained that one of his wounds – a cut that ran diagonally from Backhouse's left shoulder to the right side of his waist – could only have been inflicted by an attacker if Backhouse had remained completely still while the perfectly formed arc was cut into him: hardly a likely scenario. Also, there were no 'defence cuts' on the backs of his hands, cuts received when you attempt to ward off a thrusting or slashing knife attack.

The clincher – if one were needed – was the fact that Colyn Bedale-Taylor's right palm was covered in his own blood, which could only have got there immediately he was shot as he instinctively clutched at his chest. If Bedale-Taylor had been clutching the craft knife after he'd been shot, a portion of his right palm would have been less bloody, where the knife had been held. More likely, had he been holding the knife when he was shot, it would have fallen from his grasp as he was blasted backwards. The craft knife had obviously been placed in Bedale-Taylor's hand after his death.

The police had also uncovered additional information about Graham Backhouse that swiftly turned into a motive for engineering the whole threatening letter scenario, and much more. Their suspicions had been aroused from the moment he called the ambulance when the car bomb went off. As detectives were to reveal later, Backhouse made a serious error when he telephoned for an ambulance. He told the control centre that his wife had been injured 'in an explosion', yet, at the time, no one had mentioned to him exactly how she had been hurt, and he was not there to see the bomb-damage to the car.

Graham Backhouse was seriously in debt, owing £70,000 or so, and needed money. Just prior to the car-bomb incident he had substantially increased his wife's life insurance, from £50,000 to £100,000. Mysteriously her car had broken down and, on that April day, Graham suggested she instead took the car he had booby-trapped deliberately to murder her. Unfortunately for Backhouse, his wife had survived, and now he had a problem to ensure the police had their suspect for this attack. No one knows how he enticed Colyn Bedale-Taylor to Widden Farm on 30th April, to be murdered in cold blood, but it was planned and plotted just as all the alleged threatening

Graham Backhouse. (Western Media Publishing)

telephone calls, notes, the decapitated sheep's head and the attempt to murder his wife had been planned and plotted.

Also, unbeknown to Backhouse, an hour before Bedale-Taylor called to visit him that fatal evening, two women detective constables had been at Bedale-Taylor's home speaking with Mrs Margaret Bedale-Taylor on routine inquiries about the bombing. Detective Constables Stefanie Whittle and Heidi Brown had both seen Colyn Bedale-Taylor there, and described him as calm and relaxed, saying to his wife that he was soon off to see Graham Backhouse. He certainly had not looked like a man in a vengeful mood.

The police charged Graham Backhouse with the murder of Colyn Bedale-Taylor and the attempted murder of Margaret Backhouse. Right up to the end, he continued to try to substantiate his original story. Even in custody at Horfield Prison, he persuaded another prisoner to smuggle out an anonymous letter to the editor of the *Bristol Evening Post* stating it was Colyn Bedale-Taylor that had been responsible for the vendetta. Unfortunately for Backhouse, the power of forensic analysis stepped in once more and proved that the so-called anonymous letter had, in fact, been written in Backhouse's handwriting. The same detectives also discovered that the note pad in Backhouse's office bore the impression of the words YOU NEXT which had been written on the sheet torn off and placed with the sheep's head on the stake. Backhouse eventually stood trial at Bristol Crown Court where the whole plot was unravelled over several weeks before an incredulous public. He was found guilty and on 18th February 1985 received two life sentences.

2

LOVE, HATE AND DEATH: A BRISTOL TRAGEDY

'She was in a certain condition by another man.'

It was 1 o'clock on a chilly Monday morning at Temple Meads railway station in Bristol. It was 15th October and the year was 1917. Far from being deserted, platform five had a bustle about it as soldiers returning to the front line in France waited for the train. Wives, girlfriends and families were also there to see their loved ones off at the end of their leave. There was also a sprinkling of civilian passengers getting the early morning connection to other parts of the UK. Finally, military police were on duty to safeguard the operation of this crucial transport link in this time of war and espionage.

On platform five a Mrs Webb was working with station patrol. She had been glancing across at a soldier obviously returning to his unit and having to say farewell to his sweetheart. She was taken with the young couple's plight at parting, but also noticed that the soldier's finger was caressing the trigger of his rifle, which was slung from one shoulder by its strap. Suddenly, to her disbelief, he pulled his gun down to his right side, the butt at his hip, aimed it at his female companion and pulled the trigger. It was almost like watching in slow motion as the crack of the rifle rang out and the young woman was blasted backwards, down onto the concrete floor, shot in the stomach and groin.

Mrs Webb could not quite take in what was happening. The soldier's expression was not that of an angry man; for a moment she had thought he was being silly and playful, pretending to shoot his companion, but the echoing shot was as real as the woman lying in her own flowing blood on the station platform. She remembered a shocked silence – it must have lasted only for a second – but it seemed as if everyone had been frozen where they stood except the soldier, who had stepped back, appearing to survey what he had accomplished. From the corner of her eye she saw people running towards the spot and then everything came back to reality, screaming, shouting, and the soldier just standing back waiting as a military police officer grabbed him. As he did so, the soldier spoke. 'I have shot my wife,' he said to the arresting officer.

'SHOCKING TRAGEDY IN BRISTOL,' proclaimed the *Bristol Observer*. 'SOLDIER'S WIFE DIES FROM WOUNDS.'

The soldier was identified as 32-year-old Albert Cross of the Gloucestershire Regiment, who had been visiting his wife and children on a 10-day ticket of leave from trench warfare in France. He had clearly shot his 27-year-old wife Bessie in cold blood – 'a domestic tragedy,' concluded the first newspaper reports of the incident. Bessie had been rushed to Bristol General Hospital in what was termed 'a dying condition', and it was in that hospital that she did indeed die.

Her husband had immediately been put under arrest and held under guard in the station porter's room, and was collected by the civilian police and taken to Bedminster police station to be charged. What had not been publicised yet was Albert Cross's other comment made to the military police after he admitted to shooting his wife. By way of explanation almost, he had added that she was 'in a certain condition by another man.'

So, there were now possibly two victims to this murder, his wife and her unborn child.

Later that Monday morning, instead of being on the early morning train from Bristol en route to France, Private Cross was in the dock at Bristol Magistrates' Court to answer a charge of wilfully murdering his wife. Described by the press as being of medium stature and bronzed, Cross listened intently to the

Love, Hate and Death: A Bristol Tragedy

Temple Meads station, Bristol.

evidence of the arresting officer Lance Corporal Whitelock of the military police.

> 'I was on duty at Temple Meads railway station at 12.55 this morning,' said Whitelock, 'when I heard the sound of a rifle shot from the direction of Number 5 Platform. I proceeded there and found a soldier standing near the Superintendent's office. I approached him and he said to me, "I have shot my wife." He also said his wife was in a certain condition by another man.'

Cross was remanded in custody for one week, the scrambling newspaper reporters noting his 'air of composure throughout the brief proceedings'.

The next day, Tuesday 16th October, an afternoon inquest was opened by the City Coroner, Mr Barker, on the tragic victim, Bessie Cross.

Confirming the deceased's address as 5 Henry Row, the description of the terrible incident followed, with a local solicitor, Mr E.J. Watson, representing Private Cross. The public, alerted to the inquest and hoping to catch a glimpse of the soldier turned murderer, were disappointed he was not brought to the coroner's court. The only witness was the distressed mother of Bessie, Mrs Florence Holder, of 15 Lamb Street, St Jude's, who formally confirmed for the court that the victim was indeed her daughter and that she had been married to Albert John Cross. The inquest was then adjourned until the following Tuesday when the full details of the post-mortem would be available.

Tuesday 23rd October saw the resumption of the coroner's inquest at Bristol's Merchant Street Court. The medical evidence at the resumed inquest finally confirmed the shocking fact that there were indeed two deaths that cold Monday morning on platform 5. Bessie Cross had been six months pregnant.

It is from this moment on that a very intense, moving and remarkable story begins to unfold: an emotional journey that starts with the harsh reality of a cold-blooded murder by a husband of his wife and her unborn child, and takes us to the trenches in France and the sheer attitudinal power of wartime patriotism. This was to become a murder trial like no other, and one that would tear at the heart of the most hardened legal prosecutor.

The catalyst that revealed the real story of Albert and Bessie Cross to an avid newspaper-reading public, and to the legal process which now enveloped them in both life and in death, was discovered by plainclothes police officer William Tiler. On the Wednesday following the shooting, Tiler went to the Cross home in Henry Row, Baptist Mills, to search for any additional information that might assist the legal proceedings, evidence confirming Cross's proclaimed motive for the murder. He recovered a small bundle of letters tucked behind some photographs by the back bedroom fireplace. These letters would now play a highly significant role in Cross's fortunes – literally one of life and death. Sometimes poignant, often direct and brutal, loving yet harsh, they dominated the proceedings at both the resumed inquest and the subsequent murder trial of Albert Cross.

At the resumed inquest, it had been revealed by Mrs Elizabeth Parry, a friend of Albert and Bessie who shared the house in Henry Row, that her friend Bessie had been having a liaison with a local man, Jim King, and had been made pregnant by him. Once she became pregnant, King had written her a despicable letter condemning her sexual behaviour with him and indicating he was going to tell her husband. The bundle of letters showed that he did then write to Albert Cross, who was under fire in the trenches in France, saying 'I do not know if your wife has written to let you know of her carrying on – I have nothing to do with her since August 3rd 1917'. The letter, a copy of which was among those found in Bessie's house, continued with details of the affair and insults about his wife that must have shocked him to the core.

Albert loved Bessie unconditionally and they had two sons whom he adored. Living under appalling conditions in the midst of trench warfare, fighting for his country, he was in a mental turmoil. He steeled himself and composed a letter back to King and another to his wife. These letters would come to have a significance beyond their original purpose.

The letter to Jim King dated 23rd August 1917 was read out to a hushed coroner's inquest that dull October Tuesday afternoon:

> Just a line to let you know I am in receipt of your letter which of course is not very interesting to me. My opinion of you and my wife are a pair well met. You are trying to blame her and she is trying to blame you. If you have a family, I am sorry for them and your wife.
>
> It is me and my little boys that got to suffer but you won't get off scotch free if I can help it. You have played with my wife for eight months and now you have got her into trouble and got tired of her.
>
> You write and say it is most time I knew all about it. It seems to me, you have made a hobby of hunting up women who have their husbands serving their country, or some poor widow, and you ruin them and then cast them aside. Why don't you be a man and stand by the woman you have ruined? So far as I am concerned I only live for my poor little boys. I am finished with her but I am not going to see her ruined by a coward like you. I am her husband and I love her and I mean to protect her.

The letter was signed 'from Mr Cross whose home you have ruined'.

Clear in his letter are the emotional conflicts and dilemmas that this devastating news created for him, as well as his view of the despicable King. Cross asked for furlough, to return home to Bristol, but was told he would have to wait until October. We cannot know what thoughts were racing around his head but he composed and sent the following letter to Bessie on 6th September 1917:

> Just a line to let you know I am all right at present bar upset. Yes, I came through the battle all right and I hope I shall come home safe for the sake of the little boys. I have

had a long letter from the man who (**you say**)!! is the father of your expected child. You can see the letter I have had from him and you can see what kind of character he has given you and he says, if it were not for the children he would have given you a hiding. He says you are the worst liar he knows of and after all this you have the cheek to say you have looked after my children and loved them and you have been misconducting yourself with this man and others since last December – so he tells me. Well, I have been going through hardships out there. As regards the children, they will be far better off and will soon get used to being away from a cruel mother as you. What steps I take is what I do of my own will, you are a cruel, lying woman and I don't care if I never hear from you again. I know if I was to get knocked out, the tears you would shed would be crocodile tears. You say you can't starve, look to Mr King for pity, love for my boys xxxx

I am enclosing you a copy of the letter I wrote to Mr King at 41 Aiken Street, Barton Hill.

This powerful letter, indicating a man with a bitter heart towards his unfaithful wife, served its purpose to show Cross could be capable of murder, so distressed was he at her misconduct. Another part of the inquest's purpose was to investigate whether it was an accident rather than murder. Had it been an unfortunate mistake that a live cartridge had been left in the rifle on his return from France? Since the rifle had no 'cut off' or safety device, it could easily have been triggered in error. The possibility of accidental firing seemed remote and now, with the letter confirming his view of Bessie as a 'cruel, lying woman', the jury were becoming persuaded that Private Cross was someone who had been pushed to the limit – provoked into the murder of his wife.

Additional evidence was provided that did soften this picture a little. Up to this point no real account had yet been given that dealt with the ten days between Private Cross's arrival home from the front for the weekend of 6th October, and that fateful Monday morning departure on 15th October.

Walter Hart, an inspector from the NSPCC, had called at Albert Cross's request on Monday 9th October to discuss the future of the couple's children. Bessie confessed to the Inspector that she had been seeing another man and was now pregnant by him. Albert was concerned that his children would be better cared for away from her immoral influence. Hart told the inquest that he was impressed by Cross, who had expressed great sorrow for his wife and was obviously still very affectionate towards her despite her misbehaviour. He said he had never known a man speak so well of his wife under such circumstances. Cross had also told Hart that he had forgiven Bessie.

Mr Watson, the solicitor representing Albert Cross, asked Hart, 'Was there any resentment shown by Cross towards his wife?'

Hart replied, 'On the contrary, he expressed pleasure at again being with his wife and family and praised his wife for the way she had looked after his home and children during his absence.'

So, a really mixed emotional picture was emerging. It would seem that Cross's motive in calling in the NSPCC inspector had been to shock his wife into realising the seriousness of what she had done, and that in fact he did not want his family split. Was this the behaviour of a murderer?

The final witness to this tragic unveiling of the tangled relationships was the other man, James King of 41 Aiken Street, Barton Hill, an engineer-fitter. King admitted that he not only had written to Albert Cross and to Bessie, but also to Bessie's mother, condemning her behaviour with him. Mr Watson then elicited from King quite a remarkable story that again showed Cross as a kind and loving person, not a bitter murderer. Watson, addressing King, had asked, 'Notwithstanding the great accusation you made in the letters, did Albert Cross come and see you on October 14th, the day he was leaving for the front?'

King replied, saying, 'Yes and he asked me to come and see him and his wife and to bring my wife and I did so.' He went on to explain how he admitted to Cross that he had been 'carrying on' with Bessie for the past eight months. His own wife had been very upset; hardly surprising given that they had nine children of their own at home. Cross had told King how sorry he was for Mrs King, and made it clear that he now forgave King and they parted, King claimed, 'on the best of terms'.

It was now left to the coroner to address the jury. He railed against anyone avenging himself, no matter how powerful the provocation. This, he claimed, would make civilised society impossible. He also described King's letter to Cross as 'the most dastardly act that could be possible'.

He found Cross's forgiving attitude remarkable and referred to his 'extraordinary charity', reminding the jury that there had been no evidence of any dispute during the ten days that Cross had been at home. On the contrary, witnesses had commented how caring Cross had been towards his wife. It came down to a decision by the jury whether it was an accident or an act of deliberate murder. There was no evidence of mental aberration.

It took 30 minutes of deliberation by the jury who returned a verdict of 'Wilful Murder against Albert Cross, under Great Provocation.' The jury also added a condemnation of Jim King, unanimously agreeing that 'the conduct of King is most reprehensible, he being responsible for all the trouble and ... deserving of the severest censure'.

In response to this unusual addendum by the jury, the coroner, Mr Barker, called King forward to the witness box. With a deliberately measured and clear voice, he leaned sternly towards a nervous Jim King and said: 'You have heard the jury's censure, King. I have to say that I heartily agree. They have returned a verdict of wilful murder against Albert Cross, but there is only one man responsible for that woman's death – that man is you. Go.'

Once the coroner's verdict was announced, Albert Cross was looking at a murder trial and, it would seem, certain death by hanging. He appeared before the magistrates at Bristol Police Court on the following Tuesday, 30th October, charged with the wilful murder of his wife. The queue for seats in the public gallery ran right down the street, whilst the public jostled to get their first view of Private Albert Cross. He was wearing his khaki fatigues and looked tired, his normal bronze complexion now fading in the confines of prison remand. He made no reply to the charge of murder, but given the verdict in the coroner's court, this hearing was more of a formality in order to move to trial at the next assize.

The tragedy that took place on platform 5 of Temple Meads railway station was outlined once more, together with Mrs Webb's evidence of Cross pulling the trigger whilst aiming at Bessie from the hip. Again she mentioned that he might have been merely trying to frighten his wife and the possibility that it had been an accident. The feasibility of resurrecting this argument, however, was soon damaged when Charles Rendle, a Midland Railway Company foreman who had been on duty on platform 5, testified that Cross had told him, 'She is my wife, I shot her.' The letters previously read out at the coroner's inquest were referred to and in a very short time the prosecution had concluded what they clearly saw as a formality to enable the magistrates to commit Cross to trial.

In response to this, Albert Cross now spoke, declaring, 'I am not guilty and I wish to call evidence.' Watson, his solicitor, called Jim King to the stand and again King recalled the generosity of Cross and his forgiveness under what had been terrible circumstances for him. Watson had a clear strategy to push as hard as he could at this hearing to prevent his client going to trial as a wilful murderer. He made a long address to the Bench to make it absolutely clear that they needed to be satisfied beyond 'a mere suspicion, that "malice" and "aforethought" had been made out'. He put forward the point that this act of homicide '... might be the act of purest accident – the most innocent of acts amongst friends'. He reminded the Bench that '... the circumstances of the case were most unusual and of an arresting intensity and he must say that never in his life had he ever heard such noble acts of forgiveness as Albert Cross had displayed.' (*Bristol Observer*, 3rd November 1917, p3.)

Cross had publicly forgiven his wife, he had forgiven the man who ruined his marriage, and on that station platform at 1 o'clock that morning, he had not intended to murder his wife.

Love, Hate and Death: A Bristol Tragedy

On the contrary, it was a playful gesture, as suggested by Mrs Webb, and when he pointed the rifle at his wife he was unaware that a cartridge inadvertently was still loaded from his time in France. There was no 'cut off' on this rifle and his touch on the trigger resulted in a tragic accident. 'Did Cross, with malice aforethought malignantly raise his rifle to shoot his wife?' Mr Watson clearly felt the answer was No, he did not. The Bench did not agree, and Cross was committed to trial for wilful murder.

The newspapers had the story of a lifetime on their hands – love, deception, revenge, a man fighting for his country now fighting for his life, a cowardly rival for his wife's affections deserting her once she became pregnant. It would not have been surprising to hear boos and hissing greeting any appearance by King in the witness box, and clapping and cheers for kindly Albert Cross, a soldier widower with young children, his wife and their mother killed in a tragic accident.

In fact Cross's trial, which opened on Wednesday 21st November, almost took on that theme and instead of a dry, dusty replaying of the inquest and the magistrates' court evidence (although of course this was all repeated once more) there was palpable emotion in that room and in the faces and voices of legal counsel.

So much so that prosecuting counsel, Mr E.C.H. Weatherly, confessed that as he wished to speak calmly and clearly, he could not trust himself to read out some of the letters that had passed between Albert Cross and his wife Bessie. He was clearly telling the court that emotion would overcome him and so he delegated the task to the Clerk of the Assize.

The public gallery, packed with women, already gave forth sobs and sighs which did not take much to blossom into full-blown weeping. Two letters in particular were to change the course of Albert Cross's life as they were read to a hushed court, broken by the occasional sobbing of some tearful spectators, one of whom had to be led from the gallery.

The first was written in August by Bessie Cross to Albert, once the terrible news had come out concerning her unfaithful behaviour, her pregnancy and King's claim in his letter to Cross that she had been with other men. The letter also followed Albert's threat to leave her and take the boys away.

> I confess I have done wrong, but only with one man. This is the revenge that he said he would have. As you said, there is no forgiveness, I must go into the workhouse until I am out of my trouble ... If you are going to take my little boys away from me, that will break their little hearts and mine. I will make him suffer for this. If I go out there, I shall be out of everyone's way and all I hope is I die while I am going through it for I got nothing to live for now. All I hope that you will be happy I'm gone,
> So goodnight, Bessie, love from the children.

The impact of that letter was clearly seen in the faces of all there and when Albert Cross's reply to that letter was read out, it proved too much for some to bear and they openly cried. On 26th August he had written in reply:

> Just a line to your letter confessing your misconduct and your condition. Well, Bess you know I have not got a hard heart but I must look after the welfare of my little boys. You say I might be happy when you are gone but Bess I still love you more dearly than I can tell you. Have I not told you times we have been talking quietly how those dirty blaggards go hunting for women who have got their husbands away and what they do when they get tired of them but you would not listen to me. I have prayed to god more than once for you and the children and asked him to guide you. I hope you don't think, my dear I'm glad to hear of this because I am broken hearted. I was hoping it was not true but you confess it is true. I have taken steps to have my children taken away and you must know I have shed many a tear as well as you and the children. You see, Bess, my love, you have brought sorrow to us all – could you not see this when this dirty cur fellow was after you? Bess, if you listen to me I will be your friend as long as I live. If you knew what we have to

go through you would have gone straight but the damage is done now, all the bitter feeling won't do any good. Ask god to take care of you and I will pray for you as well Bess, try to be a different woman for the children's sake and mine.

love for my boys xxxx
Albert

This letter, said defence counsel Mr F.E. Wethered, showed what a God-fearing and clean-minded man Cross was, and that he clearly had forgiven his wife. Wethered reminded the court also that it was possible that the cartridge had been left in the rifle accidentally, and that a witness had said she thought the prisoner was acting in fun, his expression not having been that of an angry man. It was a powerful and emotional speech. Both prosecution and defence clearly had strong feelings about what a good man Cross had proven to be.

It was left to the judge, Lord Colleridge, to sum up. Commenting on the letters that contained so much to move the most callous to sympathy, he felt that sympathy was a quality that should be possible for a jury to experience. 'The law is not the cold callous indifferent matter some people would have them believe.' Lord Colleridge reminded the jury that they must nevertheless be true to the facts of the case and not turn away from what had occurred: the death by shooting of a young woman who was pregnant, and shot by her husband.

Lord Colleridge also remarked that the prisoner's letter of 26th August '... was one which any of them would have been proud to have written, whereas that from King to Cross making the allegations against the woman with whom he was actually making assignations at the time showed a depravity which was quite [the] contrary of the prisoner's letter.'

He said it was still possible that Bessie Cross's death could have been a terrible accident in a playful moment, and not even the prosecution had suggested that Albert Cross brought a loaded gun over from France with the express intention of 'destroying' his wife. Rather cleverly the judge, who appeared quite clearly on Cross's side, reminded the jury that immediately after Cross shot his wife, it had been noted by several witnesses that he did not attempt to rush to her side in distress, but indeed seemed to step back. To explain this he said:

> '... happily the feelings of soldiers with regard to death and wounds was blunted in warfare and therefore they must not apply to the prisoner, on that point, quite the same rule they would be justified in doing if he were an ordinary individual'.

This was quite a remarkable thing for a judge to have said. It seems that he wanted Cross to be a free man. A consistent theme in this trial, sometimes explicit, always implicit, was that here was a soldier engaged in deadly fighting in France and, whilst serving his country, a dastardly, cowardly married man who already had nine children of his own had taken advantage of Cross's wife in his absence. This rogue had made her pregnant only to insult and condemn her once he had learned of her condition, then written with these allegations not only to Cross himself, but also to Albert's mother.

Accident or not, after 90 minutes the jury returned a verdict of 'Not Guilty'. The applause was deafening, swiftly silenced by the court officials. Albert Cross was a free man but could never be the same man again. Did he plan to murder his wife? Was it really an accident? Would an experienced soldier like Cross accidentally walk around with a loaded rifle that carried no safety device? This was never examined very hard in the trial as no one, not even the prosecution, wanted to see him hang. They would gladly have found a way to transfer such a verdict to where they felt it belonged, and see Jim King on the gallows.

Private Cross set off back to France on the journey that had so tragically been broken short on 15th October 1917.

3

'THE CHOCOLATE BOX MURDER'

'My only chance was an emotional appeal.'

(His Honour J.D. Casswell, KC, 1929)

One of England's most eminent twentieth-century criminal defence lawyers was His Honour J.D. Casswell, KC. He claimed that, having defended around forty people, men and women, charged with murder, only five were hanged, while the rest received a lesser sentence or, indeed, were acquitted. In the adversarial 'game' of the courtroom, where defence and prosecution cross swords in front of judge and jury, it was a remarkable score for a defending lawyer.

The City of Bath in 1929 was the location of Casswell KC's first murder brief, and the case that set him on the road to achieving such a notable record for his clients. He had been practising at the Bar for some nineteen years when he was handed 'The Chocolate Box Murder'.

Much to the surprise of a desk-sergeant at London's Paddington Green police station, a dishevelled man in his early twenties limped up to the counter to announce 'I have killed my wife.' He turned out to be William Bartlett, married to Marjorie Bartlett. The two of them lived above their sweet shop in Monmouth Street, Bath – The Chocolate Box.

Bartlett claimed that a strange sensation had overtaken him whilst with his wife in the bedroom of their flat above the shop.

He heard the crash of an iron bar falling to the ground and when he tried to focus on her face, it was just a blur of red. Then he realised her head was lying in a massive pool of blood, her face beaten to a pulp. This had happened during the night of 25th October 1929 (two nights previously), and this horrific sight led to a realisation of what he had done with that iron bar, which then had set him to aimlessly wandering the streets, ending up by taking a train to London, where he finally decided to give himself up.

The limp, the sergeant noticed, was not from his hours of walking, but due to the fact that Bartlett had an artificial leg. The Bath police found what he had said to be true, and he was charged with his wife's murder.

The media immediately dubbed this case 'The Chocolate Box Murder' and it was built up to become Bath's most sensational murder case for decades. In reality, William Bartlett, even in Casswell's eyes, was '… a very miserable, simple young man'. He certainly did not appear to have any motive for killing his wife. His childhood had been a terrible one, as his parents and his sister all died of tuberculosis, and he had lost a leg as a young schoolboy when he fell and infected his knee. Three operations later, with parts of his leg being amputated each time, the complete limb had been removed. From then onwards he became very introverted, hiding in his room. Casswell claimed 'he was strange, lonely and miserable'.

His Honour J.D. Casswell, KC, in 1938.
(A Lance for Liberty, J.D. Casswell, QC)

Indeed, meeting and marrying Marjorie in the spring of 1928 was the best thing that had ever happened to him. She was also an orphan. Now, around eighteen months later, he confessed to having brutally killed her. It seemed an insane act and this could have been Casswell's defence. But was he insane?

Between them the Bartletts had sunk money that belonged to Marjorie into a childhood dream for both of them – running their own sweet shop. The problem with this ideal soon became apparent: neither of them had the least idea about how to run a business. They were literally like children 'playing shops'. In a matter of months, their capital ran out, while the income from the shop was negligible and the bills mounted up.

On the fateful day, 25th October, Marjorie Bartlett had sold some stock and fittings for a mean £11 to stave off their creditors. She took herself upstairs to rest in bed around 6.30 that evening, and William carried her up a cup of tea, then went downstairs again. A few hours later he went up to see her once more. He never revealed what she had said to him on that occasion; he would only say that she made 'some sharp remarks'.

He told Casswell, 'One side of my head went hot and the other cold. I felt as it if it was being split open. A mist came over my eyes and I don't know what happened until I heard an iron bar fall on the floor and saw it at my feet.' He then described how he saw red on the bed. At first he did not see the details of his wife's face, until he realised how badly bludgeoned she was – her features had merged into the flowing pool of blood.

This was a ferocious attack; barbaric, some papers called it. There was no sympathy in any quarter for such a cold-blooded killing of a young woman. Red mist or no red mist – William Bartlett was a murderer and deserved to hang. Casswell's job was to present the truth, which he felt might well have been insanity, but Bartlett had settled down to be a calm, collected individual, not at all like a jury's perception of an insane killer. Motive was a key point at issue.

Did William Bartlett merely want the £11 for himself, so killed his wife to get it? When he turned himself in, he had just under £3 left, and it seemed most unlikely that he had felt impelled to kill his wife, just to spend the money wandering and travelling to London. Prosecution counsel, however, reminded the jury 'but have not many murders been committed for far less?'

William Bartlett gave evidence in his own defence, sticking rigidly to the same 'mist over the eyes' story from which he never wavered. He was composed and calm and, to the jury, Casswell thought, it looked like a desperate excuse for a deliberate murderous act. Casswell's defence submission, supported by two eminent neurologists, was that his client was suffering from epilepsy. However, the prison doctor (who appeared for the prosecution) testified that Bartlett had not exhibited any signs of such an illness whilst on remand. Casswell's later brilliance as a defence advocate was glimpsed at this moment when he suggested to the prison doctor, 'If the prisoner were going to pretend to be unbalanced, would not one surely expect him to pursue that pretence while under the authorities' observation?' The doctor agreed.

But how to sum up to the jury and save his client's life was Casswell's task. He recalls:

> A young woman whose only fault, if it could be called a fault, was making 'a sharp remark', had been brutally battered to death; the evidence for the defence had been extremely meagre; and, as I had feared, I had been unable to produce any history of previous epileptic attacks. My only chance was an emotional appeal. I must arouse the sympathy of the jury for the accused. (J.D. Casswell, QC, *A Lance for Liberty*, Harrap, 1961, p60)

This is the side of murder trials the public are rarely privy to: what actually goes on 'inside' the confrontation between prosecution and defence, each charged with gaining the opposite outcome. In this case the prosecution was clear-cut and the evidence firmly on their side. Bartlett had pleaded guilty, told his story and all his defence team could attempt was to try to save his life; but how would Casswell play it, especially as the prosecution and the judge have their say after the defence's pleas for mitigation, and he expected a hostile summing-up from Judge MacKinnon?

He told the story of this troubled youth, his poor background, the death of his parents and sister, the severe trauma of his operations and the final amputation of his leg. He then went on to speak of how William Bartlett's marriage had been a shining light in his miserable life, and how much he loved Marjorie, the woman he was to batter to death with an iron bar in a fit of insanity. It was a passionate plea to the jury, ending with a quotation from Tennyson's elegy *Break, Break Break*:

> But O for the touch of a vanish'd hand,
> And the sound of a voice that is still.

For the first and, as it transpired, the only time in his career, he reduced the jury to tears. As expected, Judge MacKinnon tried to reverse this sympathetic picture back to the image of a cold-blooded killer, but the jury were swayed and returned a verdict of 'Guilty but Insane'. In the event, rightly or wrongly, William Bartlett served only a few years in Broadmoor before being released.

So, even when you know 'Whodunnit', and the murder is a terrible, bloody one with no evidence as to real motive, or in this case, proven insanity, the final arbiters – the jury – hold the trump card. In this case, that card was expertly dealt in the city of Bath by a young KC defending in his first murder trial.

4

BONDAGE AND BATHTIME IN HENLEAZE

'The bloody fool would have himself tied up.'

Behind the lace curtains of well-heeled suburbia, all kinds of mischief occurs. What happens in the privacy of their own home between two consenting adults, a married couple indeed, is their affair, or so they thought. Introduce an occasional lodger into the nest and things could change – and in this case they did in a dramatic way.

On Saturday 7th December 1946, Gilbert Kenneth Bedford – Ken to his friends – was happily lodging with the Cornocks, Ann and Cecil, at 142 Wellington Hill West in Bristol's north suburbs. Secreted in the understairs cupboard at Ann Cornock's bidding, but unbeknown to Cecil, Ken peered through a small window that gave a view into the adjoining breakfast room. Wearing a woman's dress with a padded-out bust-line was Cecil Cornock, who was gagged, and bound hand and foot over the contours of a portable washing boiler. Ann Cornock was busy beating his backside with a bamboo cane, and scolding him with the words, 'This is perfectly ridiculous, you must promise never to do this again.'

Ken just about heard Cecil's muffled reply over the swishing of the cane. 'Lower!' came the gagged response.

Cecil Cornock's secret fetish had already been divulged to Ann Cornock's sister without his knowledge, and now it had actually been witnessed by the lodger. Ann Cornock had reached a level of confidential affinity with Ken Bedford, and had already hinted that not all was 'normal' in her marriage. She told Ken that her husband would keep her short of money if she didn't do certain 'things', and invited him to creep into the understairs cupboard the next time Cecil invited her 'to play draughts in the next room'. This was the secret signal that the need to indulge his fetish was on him, and Ann Cornock had decided that Bedford should witness what she had to go through and was no longer prepared to put up with. She also told him that occasionally (in the better weather) Cecil Cornock would bid her to tie him to a tree in the local woods and then thrash him with a cane.

It is possibly misleading to refer to 25-year-old Ken Bedford merely as a lodger, for he had a perfectly good home with his elderly mother nearby at 3 Midford Road. However, in August 1946 a dramatic event occurred that was to bring him into a special relationship with Ann Cornock.

Ken Bedford had been disabled by diseased blood following an accident at a swimming pool when he was 10 years old, and he now walked with some difficulty, using sticks. He was happy in a relationship with 21-year-old Pauline Keeling, who happened to be Ann Cornock's niece. On 5th August, as they walked together after an evening out, all of a sudden Pauline collapsed in the street whilst frantically trying to catch her breath. She died a matter of hours later in hospital. The diagnosis was pulmonary oedema, a condition in which fluid accumulates in the lungs. It was a highly distressing episode and Ken Bedford was grateful for the comforting words and support offered by Ann Cornock when they met at her parents' house for the wake.

He was having difficulties with an ulcerated wound to his leg and Ann offered to assist in dressing it for him. He began visits to the Cornocks' house, and at the weekend would often sleep over on the settee, or was sometimes allocated the front bedroom. Bedford became a frequent visitor and it is clear he had a loving affection towards Ann Cornock despite being 10 years younger. This passed Cecil Cornock by, and he grudgingly accepted Bedford's presence, but he now needed to plan his masochistic bondage sessions with care lest they be found out. Besides this complication, the Cornocks had an 11-year-old son called Maurice, and it was imperative he did not catch sight of his father dressed as a woman, let alone being beaten by his mother.

So, on this particular night, with Maurice safely tucked up in bed, and the code words spoken, Ken managed to see all from the confines of the cupboard – with some difficulty, given his severe hip problems.

The 'private arrangement' over, Ken went back to his seat in the lounge, whilst Ann went upstairs with Cecil to 'run his bath'.

Eventually, she came back downstairs alone, leaving Cecil Cornock to soak his bamboo-induced weals in peace. At least, this is what Ken Bedford had understood, but Ken was fast learning that unusual activities took place at 142 Wellington Hill West, and that all was not over. Meanwhile, alone together, Ann and Ken chatted and flirted.

Physically he was frustrated not to take things further but his disability was a problem in that way. However, they were happy in each other's company and Ann claimed not to feel threatened by Ken, as she did by her husband.

The sequence of events later that evening seems to be as follows. Ann Cornock went back up to check on Cecil around 11 o'clock that evening and when she reached the bathroom, she called for Ken Bedford to come and assist her. With his two sticks, an inability to bend, and walking difficulties, he slowly made it to the bathroom.

Cecil Cornock was lying in the bath, which was full to the very top. His head was submerged and his hands firmly tied together behind him with rope. It would have been almost impossible for him to save himself once he had slipped under the water. He was very still.

Ann and Ken struggled to lift him out of the bath, as he was literally a dead weight. Ken could not sustain the necessary lift and pull action to give any useful assistance. Ann tried to instruct him how to assist her, changing ends in case the feet were easier for him to grab than the head. They virtually rolled him to the top of the bath so he crashed over the enamel lip onto the floor, Ken catching the gas flue pipe for support and breaking it off instead. Cecil Cornock's head came down on the lino with a thump. Taking off the rope, with some difficulty now as it was really wet and heavy, they dragged him out of the bathroom, along the landing, to the front bedroom.

Ann Cornock then tried artificial respiration, possibly for about three-quarters of an hour, but to no avail. Feeling weary by now, Ann said she was also feeling sick, so Bedford went downstairs to make her a cup of tea. After they had relaxed over tea, Ann decided it was time to call the ambulance and did so from a nearby call box. It was now 1 o'clock on Sunday morning. Whilst waiting for the ambulance to arrive, she thought the bath looked rather dirty so gave it a good clean.

First on the scene was Ivor Giles, a St John's Ambulance attendant, with his colleague.

The broken flue pipe can clearly be seen in the Cornocks' bathroom. (A Lance for Liberty, J.D. Casswell, QC)

They got there at 1.07 am. Ann Cornock explained how she had found her husband at 11 pm with his head under the bath water. She was careful not to involve Ken at this stage in her story of all the happenings that night. She had decided to say he only came round later that evening, when in fact he had been staying in the house since the evening of Friday 6th December. There was also the need to explain the rather long time gap between finding Cecil at 11 pm on Saturday and telephoning the ambulance at 1 am on Sunday. Waiting for two hours under such emergency conditions seemed extraordinary. This rather odd behaviour by Ann Cornock, when her husband was either in a critical or fatal condition, was taken up on the arrival of the police in the form of Police Constable Buckland and Detective Sergeant Godden around 1.25 am, followed swiftly by Dr Fells at 2 am. The ambulance men were somewhat taken aback by the fact that the victim had been moved some distance from the scene of the 'accident' to the front bedroom, before any

41

attempt to revive him had occurred. They began immediate resuscitation attempts and were joined by the doctor on his arrival who, after examining Cecil, told them to cease as death had occurred around four hours previously.

Dr Fells then inquired about the injuries to the body. Ann Cornock explained that this was caused by getting Cecil out of the bath, when, unfortunately, he fell onto the floor, the gas flue breaking off onto his legs, then his head crashing into the side of the door and finally when he was dragged along the landing and into the front bedroom. Cecil Cornock had had a rough time of it, both in and outside the bath.

PC Buckland could not understand the extraordinary emotional detachment Ann Cornock exhibited, together with the strange lack of urgency when her husband's life was at stake. Her immediate falsehood was to claim to the police officer that Ken Bedford had only called by for a chat around 10.30 pm that Saturday night, and been briefly greeted by Cecil on his way up to have a soak in the bath. She told the policemen she had chatted to Ken in the lounge then, realising Cecil had not called out for his hot drink, gone up to see him, at which point she saw that his face was under the water. In fact, she told them she found him with one leg on either side of the top edge, his head turned towards the wall and his hair under the water. She neglected to mention the rope bondage at this stage. She had tried to find a pulse, she claimed, rather than raising his head clear from the water. Only when she had turned off the Ascot water heater and pulled out the plug did she call out to Bedford to come and help her.

In a fuller statement to the police later that morning, she went on to explain her husband's unusual sexual needs and practices, such as the boiler and beating episodes, including the information that he owned a suitcase full of women's clothes secreted in the dining room. Apparently Cecil Cornock also kept a room in London where he could enjoy dressing this way, amongst other activities. The observant constable asked her about the damp skirt and jumper he had noticed in the lounge. Ann Cornock calmly explained that she had changed her clothes before going outside to telephone, as 'I didn't want to go out in damp clothes,' she explained.

Ken Bedford's statement kept to the lie of his late evening

arrival, 10.15 pm he said. He also explained that dragging Cecil into the front bedroom from the bathroom took at least an hour, which apparently did not include the 20 minutes or so to get him out of the bath itself – another extraordinary admission in an emergency. Bedford also raised crucial contradictions by saying that Ann had performed artificial respiration whilst in the bathroom, not the bedroom, and then subsequently changed this part of his story. He confirmed that she did not empty the bath, nor raise Cecil's head from the water. Eventually he produced a statement that supported Ann Cornock, but the damage had been done and the inconsistencies were now firmly on the record.

It was even more suspicious when Ann Cornock came clean about the fact that Ken Bedford had been there since Friday, rather than arriving late on Saturday night. It seemed clear to police there was at least a conspiracy here, and not a very well planned one. This conspiracy was finally confirmed when Bedford revealed why it took so long to get Cecil Cornock out of the bath: his hands had been tied behind him.

By 5 pm on 8th December Dr Fraser, honorary pathologist at Bristol Royal Infirmary, had examined the body, confirming death by drowning, and making a detailed report of the numerous lumps, bumps, bruises and clearly visible ligature marks on the body which would later form crucial court evidence.

Too many lies, inconsistencies and reactions that seemed strange if it had been a genuine accident, together with unusual injuries to her husband's body, plus the fact he was tied up in a bath full of water, inevitably led to Ann Cornock's arrest within three days of Cecil Cornock's death – she was charged with his murder. Ken Bedford's additional admission to police of kissing and cuddling Ann, and her insistence she was merely nursing his ulcerated leg (although conceding that she had possibly given him a peck on the cheek), clearly showed a crucial love interest alongside a dead husband. The detectives were even more jubilant to then discover at the house torn-up pieces of love letters between Ken and Ann. *Crime passionel* is not a defence in English law, but it seemed that is what had occurred on

Saturday 7th December behind the suburban lace curtains of this Henleaze house.

At Bristol Magistrates' Court Ann Cornock had pleaded 'Not Guilty' but, over the three-day January hearing, the prosecution revealed that there were five 'distinct abrasions' on the crown of Cecil's head consistent with him being hit with a blunt object sufficiently hard to stun him but not kill him. Did these blows to the head occur whilst in the bath with his hands tied and, possibly, his feet also? Was the stunned husband then left to slip under the water? Or, possibly, had his feet been deliberately jerked upward so his head was submerged, and because he was tied up, had he been helpless to save himself?

Once more Ken Bedford added a twist to the story when he told the court why Ann was innocent. She went up to run the bath, he said then added: 'When Mrs Cornock left the bathroom and came downstairs to me, I heard Mr Cornock talking in the bath as she was coming downstairs. He seemed to be talking through a gag and I heard Mrs Cornock say "No". She came straight down to me and I heard him still in the bath. I know definitely that Mr Cornock was perfectly all right when Mrs Cornock came down to me.'

Unfortunately for Ken, he had changed stories so often that his credibility was seriously undermined, and the latest statement was deemed inadmissible by the Director of Public Prosecutions.

On 10th January, Ann Cornock's final day at the magistrates' court, a macabre event took place. While Dr Fraser gave evidence about the injuries to Cecil Cornock's head, a life-sized plaster model of that very head was produced in court complete with black plaster bruises. Dr Fraser confirmed that the victim had been stunned by a blunt instrument. Then a wooden toy boat was produced in evidence as the likely weapon – possibly belonging to the Cornocks' son Maurice. It had been found in the bathroom by detectives. Dr Fraser disputed Ann Cornock's crashing and bumping accounts of the injuries claimed to have happened in getting Cecil out of the bath. The injuries to the body fitted an attack not a series of accidental knocks.

Cecil Cornock, Ken Bedford and Rosina Ann Cornock.
(By kind permission of the Weston & Somerset Mercury*)*

'That is untrue,' exclaimed Ann Cornock.

The hearing went on until 9.30 pm and ended with her committal to Bristol Assizes on a charge of murder.

From *The Times* to the *News of the World*, the story was a media winner: it was perfect. Kinky practices and sexual perversions, disabled lover, tied-up husband possibly attacked and drowned in the bath and then, to top it all, Mrs Rosina Ann Cornock, now in Cardiff Prison awaiting trial, was found to be two months pregnant. The fact she had made it clear that she did not have 'normal' sexual relations with Cecil left Ken to be the likely father, yet Ken claimed to be a virgin because of his disability. The plot thickened and the newspaper-reading public loved it.

Ann Cornock's defence counsel, the indefatigable J.D. Casswell, KC, had a different perspective on this case. A pregnant client on a murder charge would avoid the death penalty should she be found guilty.

Casswell also revealed that, of all his clients, he could not understand Mrs Cornock's almost unnaturally strict emotional control and lack of any sense of passion or reaction – indeed he nicknamed her 'pokerface'. He commented: 'From the time when I first saw Mrs Cornock at Horfield Prison on the evening before the trial, until the end of her protracted ordeal in court, I never saw her expression change.'

He described her thus: 'She had brown eyes set in a rather long face, quite colourless except for a slight flush over her high cheek bones and a very resolute chin.' He put her poker-faced expression down to almost fourteen years of married life with Cecil Cornock and his 'unnatural practices' – she had lost her sense of emotional response.

HUSBAND DEAD IN BATH
WIFE ON TRIAL FOR MURDER

So ran the headline in *The Times* describing the first day of the trial which began on Tuesday 4th March 1947. Bedford had escaped any charges in connection with the death of Cecil Cornock because of his disability, and the supposition that he had neither the agility nor the strength to have been involved.

Torn-up love letters carefully pieced back together by detectives formed an important part of the prosecution's case, presented to prove that the couple had had a motive for getting Ann Cornock's husband out of the way – permanently. One from Ken Bedford read: 'Dearest ... you do make me jealous ... but cannot take any risk of losing you ... I realise more and more that I could not go on without you, my dearest. You belong to me, and that knowledge gives me happiness.'

Ann's feelings towards Ken were absolutely unambiguous: '... there is only one thing I am living for and that is the day when I can say you are really mine ...'. Another ran: 'My dearest Ken ... We have to fall into one another's ways, and the sooner the better, because all lovers have differences ... belonging to each other always ...'.

Ann Cornock calmly described these as a joke: that they were teasing each other about how to write a real love letter. She explained that this was why they were never folded and sent to each other as lovers would do, but merely torn up and thrown away when the 'game' ended.

The two-hour delay in summoning assistance, the contradictions between the accounts given by Bedford and

Cornock, the love letters, her pregnancy and the forensic evidence of a possible attack on a helpless, bound victim in a bath of water formed a powerful case for the prosecution. Ann Cornock's lack of emotional response to this did not assist her image with the jury. It was clearly noticeable when Ken Bedford declared from the witness box that he was a virgin and had never had sexual intercourse with Ann Cornock. She never even glanced at him, entering or leaving the box.

The balance of the case for both prosecution and defence hung on whether Cecil Cornock's injuries, particularly to the head, occurred before or after death by drowning. Amazingly, neither the toy boat said by the prosecution to be the likely weapon of attack, nor the wet ropes said to have been used to tie Cecil up in the bath, were subjected to any detailed forensic examination. Did an unbound Cecil merely languish in a hot bath, become faint and slip under the water? The defence said it was as simple as that, but of course had no evidence to support this idea, though naturally they did produce a medical man to say it was certainly possible. The doubt, albeit small, was raised in the jury's mind. Dr Fraser, for the prosecution, however, was unambiguous and to the point:

> It is my opinion that the bruises on the dead man's head were caused while Cornock was still alive and while his heart was beating strongly; they were caused by being hit with some object and not by falling on the floor or against some solid substance.

Once more he produced the plaster head with black patches and explained all. Casswell wryly recalled, 'It was a most unpleasant sight and calculated to have the most prejudicial effect on the jury.' To counter the impression left by this exhibit and testimony, Casswell's defence witness, Dr Gibson, even went so far as to produce evidence that the bruising was not significant, by persuading a woman working in his laboratory to fall over and bruise her head, so he could judge the severity of the bruising in relation to the possibility of Cornock being bumped and falling from the bath! He also asked an assistant to tie him up tightly, wait 15 minutes and then remove the cord, so he could sit in a hot bath for 30 minutes to see the effects of ligature markings on the wrists. They were still clearly visible, so could have been left from the earlier 'session' downstairs rather than from being tied up in the bath. Dr Gibson, however, did not claim to have gone on to explore other features of the night's events in pursuit of scientific facts.

Was there reasonable doubt as to whether Ann Cornock had murdered her husband of thirteen years, Cecil Cornock? Would the jury accept that she had been confused and distressed, as she claimed, and that this explained the two-hour delay in summoning help that fatal night? In reply to the direct question, 'Did you have anything to do with your husband's death on December 7th?', she replied 'No'.

The trial lasted four days, finishing on Friday 7th March 1947, and the jury were left with a dispute between the medical witnesses as to whether significant injuries had occurred before or after drowning, and whether Ann Cornock had 'assisted' in that drowning. Was she a murderess? Approximately 75 minutes after retiring, they returned. The verdict was 'Not Guilty' – the court dissolved in uproar, and the press rushed out to file their take on such an unexpected outcome.

Apart from reporting Mrs Cornock's acquittal and immediate release from custody, *The Times* also followed up with another 'News in Brief'.

NOTICE OF MARRIAGE TO ACQUITTED WIDOW

Gilbert Kenneth Bedford, who appeared in the trial at Bristol Assizes of Mrs Rosina Ann Cornock, gave notice at Bath Register Office on Saturday [8th March] of his intention to marry Mrs Cornock who on Friday was acquitted on a charge of murdering her husband.

Soon after Mr Bedford left the register office, Mr R.A. Ingle, Mrs Cornock's solicitor, stated, 'Mrs Cornock has not seen this man alone for 3 months. She has been in prison. She has not seen him since the trial and this notice of marriage which he has given is entirely without her consent or knowledge.' (10th March 1947, p2)

Ann Cornock told a reporter: 'I am not interested in him. My friendship with Bedford is finished.'

The story that unfolded behind that particular set of suburban lace curtains was well and truly over, although left unresolved for those who really want to know the truth. Was Ken Bedford 'set up' by Ann Cornock to escape her marriage, to assist in confirming Cecil Cornock's 'accident'? Did he then, in the event, become a liability to Ann's plans to kill her husband yet make this appear accidental?

Was it an accident after all? Perhaps Cecil and Ann Cornock actually planned that Ken Bedford should be tricked into watching their kinky session, adding the spice of a secret voyeur. Maybe it all went badly wrong for Cecil and he accidentally slipped under the water and drowned, leaving Ann to play for time and make emergency plans to explain away the situation to the police? She would have needed to convince them that, thirteen years down the line, she was more of a victim than a willing participant. If it was murder, why wait so long? Even her defence lawyer had secretly puzzled over this: Casswell concluded that she did care for Cecil Cornock, despite his unwelcome demands, and that his death was an accident: 'tired by the day's events and weakened by the exertions of his revolting pleasures, he fainted in the bath. As he lost consciousness his head slipped under water.' It is important to remember that Cecil's hands were bound behind him: the day's events must have been far from over if he consented to, or required this. Ann was skilled at bondage and Ken did say Cecil '... seemed to be talking through a gag and I heard Mrs Cornock say "No".'

What did happen in the bathroom of 142 Wellington Hill West on 7th December 1946?

5

THE SIX-MINUTE TRIAL OF HANHAM WOODS

'I shot Mrs Nott.'

A shot rang out, echoing through the woods. Birds rose into the air with a frantic flapping of wings, and a blood-curdling scream pierced the morning calm.

At the sound of what was undoubtedly a woman's scream, William Nott, busy feeding his poultry close by, ran towards the noise. Within seconds another shot could be heard, but this time no scream followed. Nott arrived just as the second shot had been fired.

When he arrived at the scene, there, lying face down on the ground with her head completely shattered, was his wife Gladys. Standing a small distance away from where she lay was his neighbour Arthur Franklin. He had shot Gladys in the back and then in the head with the sporting gun he was carrying.

No sooner had William Nott taken in the horror of what had just happened, than Franklin levelled his gun at Nott and shouted, 'And you too, you rat.' Nott turned to run to his shed, a matter of feet away, to get his own gun. Wrenching open the door, he tumbled inside, pushing it shut behind him. Another shot split the air and splintered its way through the door, the bullet's trajectory slowed by the thick timber but striking William Nott in the side of his head. With blood pouring from his wound, and unable to see clearly, Nott grabbed his gun, kicked open the door and fired back at Franklin, but missed completely.

Franklin contemptuously shouted at Nott, 'I will play with you as a cat with a mouse.'

He levelled his gun and pulled the trigger. An empty click told Nott that the gun was not loaded and he lunged forward to grab Franklin, but he was in no fit state to do so. Blood was pouring from his temple and eye socket. By this time, others had arrived from their woodland homes and some men grabbed and restrained Arthur Franklin, wresting the gun from him. Others tried to see if the poor woman could be saved and another tried to stem the blood flowing from William Nott's face.

Welcome to Bath's Hanham Woods on 8th May 1935.

In these woods, various poor families scraped a living as freeholders and occasional traders in town, but on the whole this was a small, closed community, living by its own standards and morals. It was not a community that relied upon anyone else's help or values, and the police tended to leave them to their own devices. The wooden and stone shacks, scattered amongst the trees along tired dirt tracks, were not regarded as part of Bath's local community – they were outsiders.

Now, however, too much had happened to keep within the community and the police were called to deal with the murder of one of their own womenfolk.

When the police arrived, they found a distressed crowd gathered around the body of Gladys Nott, which was still bleeding from a gunshot wound to her shoulder. They had covered her head, which the second shot had completely shattered. As the pathologist would later confirm, her brain had been blown completely out of the skull and this second shot had happened after she had been felled from behind by the first of Franklin's shots.

Mrs Dyer and Mrs Taylor had quickly arrived on the scene after Franklin had realised he was out of ammunition. He acknowledged them and said, 'I have shot Gladys and I have also put a shot into Mr Nott.' He was just as open with the police, repeating his confession as soon as they arrived. Whilst Arthur Franklin was arrested and carried off to appear before Staple Hill Magistrates the following day, William Nott was taken to hospital in a very serious condition.

There was no question about Franklin's guilt, and when he appeared before the local magistrates charged with murdering

Franklin's shack in Hanham Woods. (www.bristolhistory.com)

28-year-old Mrs Bessie Gladys Nott in Hanham Woods on 8th May he openly confessed that he had done just that. William Nott was so ill, however, that Franklin had to be remanded twice whilst his neighbour recovered enough to appear at the police court to recount his version of events.

At Franklin's second remand on Thursday 16th May he was told by the Bench that they were prepared to grant him a certificate for legal aid. Franklin replied, 'I don't want one.' He was allowed to meet his brother briefly before being taken back to Horfield Prison.

Meanwhile, the tiny village of Hanham had been buzzing with the tragedy on their doorstep. People would travel down from Bristol to visit the woods and relive the dramatic events that had taken place there. Local newspapers, such as the *Bath Weekly Chronicle & Herald* and the *Gloucester Journal*, vied for sensational descriptions of this gruesome shooting, speculating on why two neighbours, living a mere 150 yards apart, had got into such a bloody feud. They had to wait until Friday 24th May to learn the truth.

I shot Mrs Nott twice in the head and, to make sure there was no feeling, I put another into her head. I then shot at William Nott but did not kill him. I hadn't another cartridge otherwise there would have been two murders.

This confession to murder and attempted murder could not have been more clearly expressed. Arthur Franklin, 45 years old, a broad stocky man with a shock of long blonde hair, stood upright and confident in the local courtroom, again refusing an offer of legal aid from the magistrates. Franklin, they learnt, was single and formerly lived in Bath with his parents, who had a grocery shop at 13 Lower Camden Place. He was now part of the small Hanham Woods community, where he had a smallholding with his brother and kept pigs. They were virtual hermits, only venturing out to collect food waste for their pigs from local canteens.

Waiting to appear in court as a witness was a heavily bandaged William Nott, who had lost his right eye completely as a result of Franklin's attack on him. The prosecution established that William and Gladys Nott were poultry farmers, had a young son, Dennis aged seven-and-a-half, and they lived around 150 yards away from the Franklin brothers and their pigs. The animosity between them had begun in November 1933 when Gladys left William and moved in with Arthur Franklin.

Every day William Nott saw his wife living with his neighbour, and looked after their son all week, sending Dennis off to school, some food scraps wrapped in newspaper to sustain him. He would dutifully take the boy to his mother every weekend, to be bathed, have his clothes mended and to have a proper Sunday meal. This went on for eighteen months, William Nott valiantly accepting the fact that his wife wanted to live with Franklin rather than with him. Then, early in May 1935, Gladys changed her mind and decided to return to William once more and live as a family. And so, on 8th May, she had made the decision to move out and was on her way down the dirt track to her old home, when Franklin walked out behind her, and aimed his sporting gun at her head. His first shot missed her head but penetrated her shoulder, hurling her to the ground, and the second shot found its target, killing her outright.

Apart from confessing what he had done, Arthur Franklin also told the police: 'I had a few words with my wife and went down to Nott's ground to get even with him. I took my single-barrelled gun with me.' It seems that, seeing Gladys walking back to his rival changed his plans, and he shot her from behind in cold blood before turning his attention to 'getting even' with his neighbour William Nott. He was asked in court if he wanted to give any reason for what he had done, but simply replied, 'I am not interested.'

It was now time for William Nott's story to be told. He was a sad figure, heavily bandaged, an eye lost to the jealous, murdering rage of his neighbour, his wife dead, and his son without a mother.

He told how he had met and married Gladys Slocombe in 1926, and that they had one son, Dennis. William had been devastated when his wife left him 18 months previously. He recalled the exact day – Tuesday 29th November 1933.

He had frequently quarrelled with Franklin about this situation and there was even a period when Gladys took furnished rooms in Bristol to try to cool the situation down. He had received a note from her saying she wanted to return, and had even visited her old home on the day before she was killed, to explain that she wanted to come back to him and Dennis. The next morning, when she had been doing just that, her life was cruelly taken.

Arthur Franklin was committed for trial at Gloucester Assizes. His refusal to accept legal aid, and his reluctance to provide any real account of his motive or personal feelings at what had happened, resulted in the trial hearing setting a record. The newspapers were full of the fact that, from his appearance in the dock until the chaplain murmured 'Amen' once the inevitable sentence of death had been pronounced by Mr Justice Macnaughton, the whole proceeding only took six minutes. This is a twentieth-century record for any murder trial in the West of England, and quite possibly the shortest twentieth-century murder trial in the whole United Kingdom.

'DOCK DRAMA LASTS 6 MINUTES' proclaimed *The Bath Weekly Chronicle & Herald*, adding that, when Franklin was asked how he pleaded, he said twice in a firm voice, 'Guilty, guilty.' It had taken only moments to outline the terrible events of that day and at the end of the trial, the same paper reported: 'Franklin, who was quite unmoved, hardly seemed to realise that the proceedings were over as he was led from the dock by warders.'

Tuesday 25th June 1935, the day of Franklin's execution at Gloucester Prison, saw unusual security measures taken outside the prison ahead of the scheduled 8 am hanging. Police had cordoned off Barrack Square to the public and were even turning back workmen who would normally pass along that way to Gloucester Docks. It had been rumoured that a well known campaigner against capital punishment, Mrs Van der Elst, would be orchestrating a mass rally in the Square, but in the event she did not do so. The two hundred or so people gathered in silence, listening to the chimes of the Cathedral bells proclaiming the hour of execution, only had nine minutes to wait before being allowed to surge forward to read the notice of execution. This stated that the hanging had been carried out by Thomas W. Pierrepoint, and was posted by a warder on the massive prison gates.

This tragic story, however, was not over with the execution of Arthur Franklin on that sunny June morning. Living alone and depressed, Franklin's brother set off one morning, stood on the edge of a rain-filled quarry and shot himself. It was a few days before he was missed and around a week before his body was found in the quarry. Years later, after his father died a broken man, Dennis Nott left Hanham Woods and married a girl from nearby Pucklechurch, where he worked on her father's farm. During hay-making, he fell from a large haystack and died from a broken neck.

Family tragedy takes many forms.

6

TRAGIC MURDERS IN
WORLE

*'I can't handle the pressure these girls
have put me under.'*

Police Constables John New and David Bradley were on
their regular patrol in the Weston area when they
received an urgent call to an incident at Cherrywood
Rise. It was Monday 8th September 1986 and a seemingly quiet
afternoon in the district of Worle. This would soon be shattered
and involve them in events that would not only change their lives
but those of many others.

Reaching the normally quiet residential area, they saw a
young man wearing a khaki and green shirt and army
camouflage trousers, clutching a shotgun. Lying on the
pavement nearby was a young girl, sprawled in a severely
injured state, with blood spilling from a gaping head wound.
Seeing the patrol car, the young man walked straight in front
of it brandishing the gun, shouting, 'I am very sorry, I'm going
to kill myself.' With that he placed the gun barrel into his
mouth.

Instantly the police officers worked as a team to prevent his
intended suicide, one advising him to stay calm and hand over
the weapon, the other borrowing a cigarette from a neighbour
to offer the young man in exchange for the gun. It was essential
to wrest the gun from his possession, as he was clearly
unpredictable and might turn on anyone at all and kill them. At
that moment another car arrived.

Frantic with worry, it was Jim Hastings and his son Andrew.

Jim had been told that his daughter was injured and lying in the street. He drove past the young man with the shotgun, who he instantly recognised as Dean Westwood. Westwood had been dating his daughter Karen. Then Jim saw Karen's limp body on the pavement and knew the worst. He turned to his son and said, 'He's killed her.'

In a moment, Andrew Hastings leapt out of the car, fury in his actions as he attempted to attack Westwood with a wooden spirit level, but the two constables held him back. Jim grabbed his son and, as distraught as he was, hissed urgently that he'd lost one of his children and did not want to lose another. Jim knew how arrogant Dean was, hating the way he had paraded through the Hastings house boasting about himself every time he came to see Karen. 'He used to strut around as if he owned the place, and sprawled in the chairs as if he was king,' Jim would later recall.

PCs Bradley and New worked hard, talking to Westwood, pleading with him to hand over the shotgun. He refused. After more persuasion, Westwood agreed to give himself up, but kept a firm grip on the shotgun. Walking with the constables to the back of the police car, Westwood held the gun in front of him and broke it open, ejecting a live cartridge. The police car's boot was raised and steadily, guided by the careful words of the officers, Westwood placed the gun inside the boot. John New quickly closed the boot, Westwood calmly accepted his arrest and was taken to Weston police station.

What had actually happened that afternoon was even more terrible than anyone could have imagined. The previous day, Sunday 7th September, Dean Westwood, who was 21 years old, had been severely agitated about the ending of a six-week relationship with 19-year-old Karen Hastings, a bubbly, extrovert character, much loved by the elderly folk in the residential home where she worked as an auxiliary nurse. She also worked as a barmaid in a local pub – Mr B's – and as it was a Sunday, her night off, she had decided to spend it having fun with her best friend, Mandy Cottom, an 18-year-old girl who worked as a cook at the same pub. Dean Westwood had been brooding over the end of the relationship, and tracked the

Dean Westwood. (By kind permission of the Weston & Somerset Mercury)

girls down to the Smuggler's Inn on the seafront, then later to Mr B's, seeing them enjoying themselves, which he resented. He blamed Mandy Cottom for the split, feeling (as he later said) that she had put Karen up to it.

Dean Westwood had confronted Karen Hastings, who had told him in no uncertain terms that their relationship was over. He brooded all night over how to get his revenge on Mandy, as well as on Karen for rejecting him. On the following morning, Monday 8th September, he wrote a chilling confession to a crime that had not yet occurred but had been played over and over again in his mind.

> *To whom it may concern*
> *I Dean Westwood do hereby admit to Shooting Mandy and Karen Dead, due to Constantly having the ——— taken out of me and also being treated like ——— (by them!) I would like to apologise for my actions but don't regret it.*
> *they both say I'm a nutcase so I may as well act like one if they think I am!*
> *I can assure you I am not a nutcase but I can't handle the pressure that these girls have put me under*
> *Yours sincerely*

He then signed his name.

Cherrywood Rise.

Putting on his army-style clothes, he took the note, together with his father's single-bore shotgun, put a Bowie knife in his pocket and set off to visit his only real friend, Darren Owens. No doubt, he decided to take the Bowie knife as well to ensure death was the end result, should the shotgun not complete his horrific plan. He told Owens exactly what he intended to do – shoot both girls dead. His friend did not believe him and Westwood left without managing to convince the young man that he really meant it. He had hoped that Darren Owens would hold the note for him, and pass it on to the police once his plan had been carried out.

Next, Westwood went to confront his former girlfriend and her best friend, and found them both at Karen's home in Cherrywood Rise. They shouted at him to leave and to stop making a nuisance of himself – he was not wanted there. He did leave, but only to return to his car.

In the car was the shotgun, which he assembled and loaded as he made his way back to the house. It is difficult to imagine the terror both girls endured when confronted by an armed Dean Westwood. They screamed and Mandy Cottom ran into the

POLICE OFFICERS PRAISED

Police Constables David Bradley and John New. (By kind permission of the Weston & Somerset Mercury)

kitchen, trying to escape through the back door. Westwood calmly strode after her, raised the gun, and shot her in the head. She died instantly.

Karen Hastings was hysterical and scrambled to barricade herself in the living room. With no sense of anything other than killing on his mind, Dean Westwood smashed the glass panel above the living room door, and pushed the shotgun through the hole in the jagged glass. Karen could only scream as the barrel waved in the air above her head. She flung open the door, pushing hard at Westwood, to get past and flee the house. They struggled briefly in the hallway, until she managed to break loose and head for the kitchen, where her friend Mandy lay dead. Westwood was a man possessed and caught her, the gun exploding in his hand as he misfired into the kitchen wall.

This was Karen's chance and, unlike Mandy Cottom, she did manage to escape out of the back door and into Cherrywood Rise.

Westwood did not panic but calmly reloaded the gun as he followed her fleeing down into Cherrywood Road. He took aim and shot her in the head. The later medical evidence described how the impact of the shot, passing through her skull, sliced the top of her head away. Karen, like Mandy, died instantly.

With Mandy lying dead in the kitchen and now Karen murdered outside her home, we return to the moment that Police Constables New and Bradley, totally unaware of the full horror of what had occurred, confronted Dean Westwood striding about in his camouflage costume. Two murders of the most despicable nature under his belt, another one or two would have made no difference to him at this stage. Talking Westwood down, and securing his arrest, quite rightly earned both officers a later commendation for bravery from the Chief Constable of Avon.

Now lives were shattered: Jim and Margaret Hastings and son Andrew; John and Valerie Cottom with daughters Wendy and Tracey – happy, close families blown into a world of grief by one man and his obsessive personality disorder. Karen Hastings and Mandy Cottom – inseparable friends – had been planning a holiday in Tenerife, having enjoyed a fine time three months beforehand in Cyprus; murdered, and to what purpose? Westwood's mother and father, equally shattered by their son's action, were left the following note by Dean:

> *Dear Mom and Dad,*
> *I am sorry things had to end this way, but in a million years you would never understand the pressure I have been under through women amongst other things.*
> *I love you very much and I beg you not to be upset or hate me for what I have done.*
> *I love you all*
> *Dean*

Now, charged with the murder of two teenage girls, Dean Westwood became what many people said he had always longed to be, the centre of attention. Standing in court and pleading 'Not Guilty' to a double murder planned and executed on that September day was guaranteed to bring him attention, as well as more anger at his arrogant and cold-blooded attitude towards his crime.

Also, this was not the first time that Dean Westwood had made the headlines in Weston for extreme violence. He had stood in the same dock in February 1985, and been sentenced to fifteen months' youth custody. Just a few days before Christmas 1984, he had carried out a vicious assault on Brian Rees, a

Weston Me

SOMERSET AND AVON HE

1986

No. 6842 (Established 1843 — Over 140 years o

TWENTY-ONE-YEAR-OLD ACCUS

Weston m
charged
two mur

CHARGED with the double murder of two teenage girls at Worle, a 21-year-old Weston man was remanded in custody until today.

Girls died

TWO teenage girls died from head injuries due to shotgun

The headlines, 12th September 1986.
(By kind permission of the Weston & Somerset Mercury)

rnry

.D

/ice)

INLAND POSTAGE 40p

Price 17p

D OF KILLING TEENAGERS

n is

vith

ers

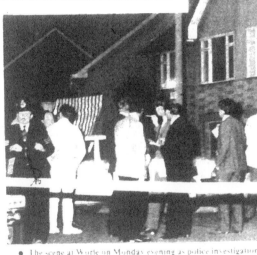

● The scene at Worle on Monday evening as police investigations continued

rom head injuries

rned the head Cherrywood Road with fatal head s and Rise ties with

British Rail guard. Mr Rees spent four days in hospital and required 28 stitches to facial wounds. Westwood had admitted to this crime, claiming in explanation that he had been drunk and depressed and wished to kill himself, but instead carried out this mindless attack on Mr Rees. After the shooting in Cherrywood Rise, he had proclaimed to Constables Bradley and New that he was depressed and wished to kill himself, putting the gun into his mouth, but once again this had been a means of gaining attention, putting the spotlight on poor, misunderstood Dean Westwood, and part of his plan.

Similarly, his school behaviour had been disruptive, according to fellow pupils and teachers. Fights would break out as Westwood demanded attention. On leaving school he had joined the army, and it seemed that he felt at home there, being given the position of batman to the Regimental Sergeant Major. However, depression, suicide attempts including wrist-cutting and drinking metal polish, and an assault on a police officer in London, together with that on Mr Rees, led to his discharge from the army. This had put him back in his Weston haunts where he eventually met and became obsessed with Karen Hastings, despising Mandy Cottom for being in the way. The day he called at number 1 Cherrywood Rise, the girls could not possibly have realised the consequences of sending him away, or of telling him not to be a nuisance. Dean Westwood knew the ill-fated six-week relationship was over and had already made the decision to end it with a double murder.

The trial of Dean Westwood at Bristol Crown Court in May 1987 revealed the depth of what was termed by the prosecution as 'a personality disorder that could leave him dangerous until his 40s'.

This might seem a strange calculation of how long he could be perceived as dangerous, but clearly it was intended to guide the judge as to the length of the sentence that should be imposed. To the anger of the victims' families, however, although Westwood was sentenced to life imprisonment for each charge of murder, the two sentences were to run concurrently. Karen's mother was reported as saying, 'I was surprised the sentences ran concurrently rather than consecutively, it's not enough. I had to come to court to see his face, I never want to see it again.' Jim Hastings added, 'He should stay in there until he dies, he is dangerous and will always be dangerous.'

These are the wholly understandable and heartfelt comments of the mother and father of a teenage victim of a vicious murder. More telling and more chilling is another comment, made around nineteen months before Dean Westwood became a double murderer. They were made by Judge Sir Ian Lewis in February 1985, when he sentenced Westwood to fifteen months' youth custody for the attack on Mr Rees. The judge said to Westwood, 'When you have served your sentence, do not be so foolish as to try to take a young life, there is a future for you.'

If only.

7

HOW NOT TO MURDER YOUR FATHER-IN-LAW

'If you find a bruise on the back of the head,
that is where his head hit the floor when I pulled
him from the oven.'

It was a blustery but not unpleasant day in mid-November 1933. Police Constable Amos knew his Bath beat well, and most people he passed acknowledged him. He would peer into driveways and alleyways 'just checking,' he'd say, 'that all is well'. Traditional beat policing at its best. He had now reached Bloomfield Road which curved up to an incline. Up ahead was a parked car he did not recognise with a lone man sitting in it whom he also did not recognise. As was his practice, he'd have a friendly word, 'just checking, you understand'.

Whilst PC Amos was speaking with the man smoking his pipe in the car, an elderly gentleman passed by on the pavement, struggling to make progress up the hill.

The driver of the car, who had introduced himself to the constable as Mr Hinks, remarked, 'The old gentleman is out for a ten-mile walk.'

The remark was made in the manner of someone who knew the old man's purpose, but not the old man himself. Hinks went on to add that he was following him in the car, as the old man had wandered off before and needed looking after.

'Won't they certify the old chap?' PC Amos asked.

'No,' said Hinks, 'he is not suicidal. The doctors say it is senile decay.'

They both watched the elderly man totter precariously ahead by forty or fifty yards or so. Hinks was just adding the information that the gentleman was 81 years old, when they saw his legs give out from under him and he fell heavily to the pavement. A passer-by stopped and helped him to his feet, the constable went ahead to check the old man was not hurt, and Hinks drove up the hill to collect him in the car. Only then did he explain that this gentleman was in fact his father-in-law, James Pullen, and that he would now take him home for a rest. No one need worry. PC Amos, however, had already made a full note of the incident, which would later prove how important 'just checking' can be.

The 'ten-mile walk' incident happened on 14th November. Sixteen days later, on Thursday 30th November, the police would meet Reginald Hinks once more. He was 32, an unemployed vacuum-cleaner salesman (he preferred to call himself an electrical engineer); his wife Constance was a divorcee with a young child, and his father-in-law James Pullen, a retired master tailor, shared the family home: Wallasey in Englishcombe Lane, Bath. It was James Pullen's weekly bath night, when Hinks would shave and bath his rather confused elderly father-in-law. According to Connie, her husband was 'kindness itself'.

This particularly bath night had gone badly wrong, for he had had to call urgently down to Connie to come and assist him. He had only left the bathroom for a few minutes, to fetch his father-in-law some clean clothes, but when he got back Pullen's head was under the water. Reginald and Connie emptied the bath, sat James Pullen upright, and wrapped him in a towel and blanket. His face had turned black and he appeared unconscious. Connie massaged her father's heart and requested her husband to fetch a doctor urgently.

Rather than telephone from a nearby call-box, Reginald Hinks decided to flag down a passing car to take him to Mr Pullen's doctor in person, a twenty-minute ride. Dr Scott Reid was out, but his wife allowed Hinks to telephone from there for an ambulance. With the ambulance on its way, he asked Dr Scott Reid's neighbour for a lift back to Englishcombe Lane,

Reginald Hinks.

explaining to the gentleman who answered the door that there had been an incident at his home, Wallasey: his elderly father-in-law had had a serious accident. They arrived just as two ambulance men had been let in by Connie and rushed upstairs to discover James Pullen sitting in the empty bath, wrapped in a towel and blanket, but unperturbed, looking hale and hearty. Meanwhile, Hinks's Good Samaritan driver was waiting outside to greet Police Constable Ford, who had been called to this possibly fatal accident.

PC Ford was surprised to see Chief Constable Mr Nelson Ashton waiting for him when he arrived shortly after 8 pm. Unbeknown to Hinks it was the Chief Constable upon whose door he had knocked to ask for a lift. They went up to the bathroom where Mr Ashton revealed his identify to a startled Hinks and suggested Pullen should be tucked up in bed. 'It's cold,' murmured the elderly man. By the time they got him into bed, Hinks had disappeared outside to wait for the doctor.

Dr Charles Gibson had been summoned by the Ambulance Service to attend an elderly gentleman black in the face after a bathtime accident. Reginald Hinks met him in the driveway, introduced himself and said there was no longer any need for him to attend, the patient having quite recovered. Indeed, added Hinks, he was sitting up in bed and calling for his supper. Dr Gibson explained he was obliged to attend an emergency call and went upstairs to see the patient. He noted that James Pullen had a good colour for an elderly man, and that there was no sign of any blackness to the face.

As the doctor reached toward Pullen with his right hand, to feel his pulse, Pullen pulled away saying, 'Don't burn me doctor, oh, don't burn me.' The doctor took this as a sign of mental confusion in the patient. Being cold when you are elderly can feel like being burnt. He reassured James Pullen that he was there to help him. The doctor examined his heart and was surprised how very strong it was for an 81-year-old.

'The sounds were perfectly regular as well as a good tone,' he noted. He examined the lungs and found no evidence of inhaled bath water.

Hinks anxiously watched the examination, remarking to the doctor he was concerned about his father-in-law's weak heart. Dr Gibson told him that, on the contrary, James Pullen had a very good heart.

Reginald Hinks then told the doctor that Pullen had a double rupture and did not have his truss on at the moment. He asked Gibson if it would be dangerous not to put the truss back on, what might happen?

The doctor explained that, if Pullen did not get up and was not made to walk any distance, his father-in-law would be fine until tomorrow, but to make sure he should put the truss on. If he were allowed to walk around without it, he might incur a strangulated intestine, which would be likely to turn gangrenous and could be fatal. Hinks promised to put the truss back on for his father-in-law. The doctor left, puzzled that he found no signs of shock whatever, given the serious nature of the accident as reported by Hinks. A good result, however: a healthy 81-year-old with a good few years yet ahead of him.

It was not long before the emergency services found themselves back at Wallasey. The very next day, in fact, Friday 1st December, two members of the Bath Fire Brigade rushed to the house as a result of another emergency call by Reginald Hinks just before 8 pm. Hinks led them to the kitchen where they saw an elderly gentleman lying on the floor about a foot from the gas stove. He had a hot water bottle propped up at his side. Hinks told Fireman Hall as soon as he arrived, 'He's gassed himself.' The firemen immediately started resuscitation procedures but it seemed clear that the old gentleman was dead. Once more PC Ford arrived at the house. Hinks, dressed in his pyjamas and dressing gown, requested, 'Don't make too much noise, the baby is upstairs.' PC Ford watched the firemen's valiant resuscitation attempts but to no avail.

'Poor old chap,' said Hinks, 'is he coming round?'

PC Ford asked what had happened. Hinks told him, 'It's my wife's father. He said he was going to the lavatory. When I found he was gone for 25 minutes, I went to look for him and I found him lying on his left side with his head and shoulders in the gas oven.' He added that his wife was at the cinema, saying to the police officer, 'I don't want my wife to know this has happened, she will go off into a dead faint.' With the new-found knowledge learned from Dr Gibson's visit, Hinks told the firemen, who were administering oxygen to James Pullen, 'You can give him plenty of gas, the old chap has a strong heart, he is very strong.' Unfortunately for James Pullen he had already had plenty of gas, but it had been carbon monoxide and was fatal. At 8.15 pm, PC Ford went to telephone for Dr Gibson, who said he would come if he could not get hold of Dr Pullen's own GP, Dr Scott Reid.

Ford returned to question Reginald Hinks about the events of that evening. Hinks replied:

> I could see what had happened, and I caught hold of his two feet, and pulled him out. You might find a bruise on the back of the head where his head hit the floor. I then placed a hot-water bottle on his heart and started to massage him and applied artificial respiration. I don't know much about artificial respiration but I rubbed him and after a few minutes I lifted his head and found it dropped back. I then telephoned for the ambulance, I knew just what to do as I called them last night and I asked them to send a policeman.

When it seemed clear the firemen could do no more, Hinks said to them, 'He may come round, as he was still gurgling when I sent for you. He was black in the face last night when I found him in the bath.'

At 8.35 pm, Dr Scott Reid arrived and, walking around the firemen who were kneeling beside Pullen, pressed his hand on the old man's chest, then examined him and said 'You can't do any more for him,' and suggested his removal to the city mortuary.

Hinks added, 'Yes, do, I don't want him here for the wife to see, she is only a little thing and, like her father, very mental.' He wanted the doctor to stay until Connie had come home, but Dr Scott Reid left with PC Ford for a private talk. Ford returned at just after 9 pm to ask Reginald Hinks for a full statement, which he agreed to provide. The police officer wrote down the statement with Hinks sitting by the fire in the sitting room eating his supper. In the kitchen, arrangements were made to remove James Pullen to the mortuary. Satisfied that he had enough information for now, PC Ford took his leave; Hinks wanted him to stay to explain things to his wife, but the constable declined. Hinks then said, 'I am sorry about the old chap. If you find a bruise on the back of the head, that is where his head hit the floor when I pulled him from the oven.' Ford left Wallasey, a little bemused that Hinks did not appear upset at the death of his father-in-law.

What inevitably had to follow such an episode was a thorough inquest into how James Pullen had met his death. Mr G.R. Paling, solicitor for the Director of Public Prosecutions, expressed the situation perfectly: 'There were two alternatives, either that Pullen died by his own action or by being put in the oven by someone else.'

The inquest opened on Tuesday 5th December 1933 and, so serious was the matter of answering that question correctly, that it required eight full days scattered across the calendar, finally reaching its verdict on Friday 19th January 1934. According to his son-in-law, James Pullen had often threatened to kill himself and had now finally managed to do so by gassing himself during the 25 minutes that had elapsed between saying he was going to the lavatory, leaving the sitting-room where he had been listening to the radio, and Hinks going to look for him and finding him in the gas oven.

What so exercised Dr Scott Reid, PC Ford and Chief Constable Ashton, and formed the centre-piece of the inquest, were the twin questions of how capable James Pullen had been of organising his own suicide, and why he might have wished to kill himself? In this incident, a very confused elderly man not only had apparently managed to put his head and shoulders in the oven whilst lying on his back – a difficult enough feat for a younger, fitter man with full mental faculties – but also had understood how to turn on a difficult configuration of two different gas-taps – top and bottom – whilst ensuring overcoats were draped effectively around the oven opening to block escaping gas. According to Hinks, he had even held two aprons in front of his face to further block gas escaping. To get inside the oven would necessitate removal of the shelves. It seemed Pullen had also taken the opportunity of placing the dog's mat carefully inside the oven to lay his head on – a mat which Hinks had removed after pulling Mr Pullen out by the legs – and placing back on the far side of the room, ready once more for the dog to sit on. Why was it not left in the oven where supposedly James Pullen had placed it? The draped coats were tidily removed rather than flung to one side as one might expect to happen in such an emergency. In fact, one overcoat was folded neatly inside the other, next to the two aprons on a nearby chair.

Neither PC Ford, Dr Scott Reid nor Fireman Hall had noticed any significant smell of gas, either on the coats used to drape around the stove, or indeed on James Pullen himself. It was a real puzzle. If the smell had been there it had long drifted away. When had James Pullen died? Hinks had said to the firemen, '... he was still gurgling when I sent for you', so if this statement were accepted, the smell of gas should have been at least uncomfortable, yet no one could smell it except for the doctor who detected a faint odour on James Pullen's mouth. If Pullen did not place himself in the oven intending his death, who did?

It was discovered by the pathologists that there was indeed a bruise on the back of Pullen's head, as kindly advised by Reginald Hinks.

A significant problem with the explanation offered by Hinks, that the bruising occurred '... where his head hit the floor when I pulled him from the oven', was that a bruise of the nature discovered could only develop in that way in living tissue. It was a bruise sustained before death, not after death. It was also indicative of a heavy blow to the head, enough to stun Pullen but not make him unconscious. So, it was also significant that Hinks wished to explain away a bruise before it had even been discovered.

Why would Reginald Hinks wish to murder his father-in-law? He had married James Pullen's daughter Constance Jeffreys on

18th March 1933. She had a six-year-old daughter, Beryl, from her previous marriage. Connie saw Reginald Hinks as a kind and wonderful man, as evidenced by taking over care of her father.

James Pullen had become confused since his wife died in January 1932, getting worse as the year wore on. Special 24-hour nursing care that had been put in place over the year, with Mr Strange, a night nurse, and Mrs Smith, responsible for day-time care, working the clock round. As Connie saw it, Reginald loved her father so much, that he dismissed the nurses in July 1933 to take over the care himself. Apparently Hinks said he would save money, and ought to take over the care: it was his father-in-law after all.

He would also assist James Pullen to redraw his will, to make certain decisions about properties he owned in Dorking, and arrange some money for Hinks himself as a 'marriage settlement'. However, his frequent attempts to take over James Pullen's monetary affairs were, on the whole, thwarted by Pullen's vigilant solicitors, who required certain medical details and legal safeguards that Hinks was unable to overcome. He had lied in a letter that Dr Scott Reid thought Mr Pullen fit enough to add a codicil to his will in favour of Reginald Hinks. So concerned were James Pullen's solicitors and Dr Scott Reid that they arranged for the Official Solicitor to take over responsibility for Pullen's estate until he died, after which it would be left to his daughter Constance in a new will.

Shortly after his marriage, however, Hinks had managed to sell one of James Pullen's properties. He had gone to Dorking, seen solicitors there saying he had Pullen's authority, and got away with it. A cheque for £900 was signed over to Hinks by Connie, who had asked her father to endorse it to her. It was money used, in some fairness to Hinks, to move from the original Pullen home in Milton Avenue to a smaller property in Englishcombe Lane where they now lived, and to buy a new car, some furniture and have some left to spend. The sale of the older, bigger Milton Avenue property, of course, put more money into the bank for Connie to access on Hinks's behalf.

Reginald Hinks painted a picture of a father-in-law who, on the one hand, was very tottery and kept falling down and bruising himself, getting up with difficulty, wandering off and becoming disorientated; but on the other hand, was capable of planning, and successfully executing, quite an intricate suicide. Regarding the former, Hinks said to the coroner:

> At Wallasey, about three weeks before he died, he fell down thirteen stairs bruising his hip and injuring his eye. A week later he fell over the gate post. About ten children gathered round, and Mrs Hinks and I carried him in unconscious – he soon came round and we did not send for a doctor. His falls were frequent and got to two or three a day.

In fact, Hinks claimed, James Pullen bumped the back of his head heavily on the sideboard on the very morning of his death, trying to get hold of some bananas.

> He was left in the dining room with the little girl while I and Mrs Hinks were washing up in the scullery. While we were doing so, the little girl ran out and said, 'Grandpa has got one of the bananas from the sideboard.' Whilst she was there we heard a bump, Mr Pullen had fallen down. I ran in, he was on the floor and the chair was tipped up and a banana was on the floor. He said, 'Oh my head, I have bumped my head.' He was dazed, and after a while he sat down quiet.
> He could not get up and my wife and I lifted him up.

This was of course a very convenient story for Hinks to recall on the last day of the inquest, because the medical evidence to the coroner was quite unambiguous: James Pullen had received a very heavy blow to the back of the head prior to his death in the oven. A morning sideboard accident on 1st December, using Hinks's six-year-old step-daughter to create greater authenticity, would now take care of any questions relating to bruising prior to death, he hoped. The problem for Hinks is that medical evidence timed the bruise as occurring one or two hours prior to death, not any earlier. It was clear the police considered Hinks had given Pullen a deliberate blow to the head that evening, enough to stun Pullen ready to place into the oven and fake his suicide.

Also of interest to the inquest was the unfortunate episode for Hinks of his lift back to Wallasey with the Chief Constable on the evening of 30th November. At the inquest Nelson Ashton was able to ask Hinks, 'Do you remember telling me on the way back that he was black in the face and by the time you got there you expected him to be gone?'

'No,' replied Hinks.

But, as well as playing up his mental frailty, Reginald Hinks also wished the inquest jury to believe that James Pullen was a man tired of life, thinking he was a nuisance to his daughter. 'He asked her to see to his business,' Hinks said. 'As long as he was well fed and clothed and comfortable, he did not want to be bothered with business.' Hinks said Pullen had definitely been a man capable of planning his own suicide, of understanding how to operate the cooker gas-taps, of knowing how to strategically place the coats and aprons and then crawl in on his back to wedge his head and shoulders inside an oven that stood around seven inches from the ground on metal legs. The Chief Constable had tried to do all this himself, not at all successfully.

Hinks disagreed with the impression this statement gave, and said to the inquest, 'I can get my shoulders in the oven, I've tried it, I've got a photograph of it.' He even knew the measurement from oven to floor, claiming it was seven-and-a-half inches, which apparently was why Pullen's head had received such a bump. He was sorry to have hurt his father-in-law on pulling him from the oven, claiming that James Pullen was still alive at that point.

At the end of a long inquest, the jury returned at 8.13 pm with their verdict, which was 'Wilful Murder, death caused by gas poisoning accelerated by a severe blow on the head shortly before death administered by Reginald Ivor Hinks.' Over the eight days of hearings, the crowds inside and waiting outside had grown each day until over 400 people were in attendance.

It was a sensational verdict to which Hinks replied, 'What a shame, what a shame.'

The coroner, addressing him, said: 'You stand committed to take your trial at the next Assizes for the county of Somerset, or elsewhere as may be directed, for the murder of James Pullen.'

Hinks, with the Chief Constable now at his side holding one arm, replied, 'Whatever for, Sir, whatever for?'

With eight inquest sessions behind him since 5th December, Hinks could look forward to an immediate magistrates' court hearing that very Saturday morning to be formally charged with murder on a Coroner's Warrant. This was followed by no fewer than three Bath Police Court hearings during February and by 16th February he was committed for trial at the Central Criminal Court. The trial proper began on 6th March 1934, Hinks pleading 'Not Guilty'. Very large crowds attended the beginning and the end of the trial on Saturday 10th March. The whole story, now well rehearsed, was repeated except this time Hinks was really fighting for his life, and he showed some temper, and yet more ill-judged comments.

Connie Hinks stood by him all the time (between many dramatic fainting episodes). The decision to bring the very stove into the court on the shoulders of five police officers brought the strongest objection from Reginald Hinks who said, 'Before my wife is called will you do her the kindness and courtesy of having that gas stove taken from the table and put under the table? I know her state of health perfectly, like I did Mr Pullen's. She fainted at the police court when she saw it. She will collapse today if she sees it.'

Even in this plea, he had carefully included the murder victim, but in a caring way. One damning additional piece of evidence that came out during these hearings was a letter dated 27th December that Hinks had written to Mr Strange, James Pullen's former night nurse. Mr Strange had consistently maintained that James Pullen had been too feeble and confused to dress himself, or indeed have any clear consecutive thought process. He also had never threatened suicide as far as Mr Strange could recall. This was a problem for Hinks because the other carer, Mrs Smith, had testified the opposite, supporting Hinks in saying that James Pullen had been mischievous, able to dress, wander about, fetch and hang up his coat, and that he had often threatened to end his life by '... throwing himself in the millpond at Dorking' or 'cutting his throat'– albeit with a pencil!

The letter read out in court was as follows:

> Mrs Hinks has asked me to drop you a line. Both she and I would like to see you again before the next sitting of the adjourned inquest.
>
> He (Mr Pullen) was always allowed to go to the lavatory by himself, and that is a statement I want you to write out for Mrs Hinks at our house when you call.

Strange never did call and supply such information. Did Mrs Smith have a similar meeting with the Hinkses in December? It was never revealed if she did so. When Strange did not cooperate, Hinks claimed that his dismissal in July had been because he frightened Connie Hinks by engaging in spiritualism, saying tappings she heard on the wall were her mother's spirit calling her. He further claimed Connie Hinks had said to him, 'The only remedy is to give Mr Strange up, sacrificing your business and being here with me and my father to look after us.'

Kindly Reginald Hinks had no difficulty 'sacrificing his business' as an unemployed vacuum-cleaner salesman to live off James Pullen's money.

Unfortunately, on three occasions different reasons had been given for the dismissal of Pullen's nurses. First, the reason claimed was to save money now that Hinks could do the job. Then, it had been because they had all had enough of the stress of James Pullen's threats and suicide attempts. Lastly, because Strange was frightening Connie Hinks with spiritualism, Reginald Hinks had had to dismiss him.

To undermine Hinks's constant claim to have been fond of James Pullen, evidence was heard from two men who had fitted a wireless aerial to Wallasey under Reginald Hinks's instruction during November, who testified that he had said to them, 'I wish the old b***** was out of the way.' Hinks denied this, but of course the wireless aerial men had no reason to lie.

Hinks's defence team sought to emphasise that James Pullen's character had been wilful: 'An old man of moods', selfish, cunning, using trickery to get his own way and 'often threatening to take his own life, capable of turning on gas-taps'. It was not going to work, since the whole argument concerning the bruising prior to death, and the clear evidence that Pullen had no ability to engage in planning and consecutive thought processes, left only one conclusion, that Hinks planned and executed the cold-blooded murder of his father-in-law. But why? His wife, Connie, would have inherited everything anyway; he had only to be patient. She loved him and he would have gained it all.

Let us not forget PC Amos, the diligent beat officer with his trusty notebook, who recalled a key admission made by Reginald Hinks the previous November whilst sitting in his car watching an elderly man with a double hernia attempt a ten-mile walk. On PC Amos asking whether James Pullen was likely to be certified, Hinks had replied, 'He is not suicidal. The doctors say it is senile decay.'

The jury retired, requesting 40 minutes later to have the gas stove brought in to them. Within 90 minutes they returned with a unanimous 'Guilty' verdict, at which point three female jurors burst into tears.

Hinks was asked if he had anything to say, to which he replied: 'Yes my Lord, I should like to say just a little sentence. I loved my home, my wife, my baby and Mr Pullen too much to wish to do them any injury at all. The verdict of the jury is not correct. It can't possibly be.' Hinks was then sentenced to death.

In the middle of April 1934 Reginald Hinks's lawyers mounted an appeal, on the basis that the detailed medical evidence had not been given enough weight by the judge in his summing-up to the jury. This came to nothing: the verdict was upheld.

On Wednesday 2nd May, the night before his execution at Horfield Prison, he embraced his wife as she departed with the words, 'Look back and give me a smile, Connie.' At 8 o'clock

REGINALD HINKS

Court Dismisses Appeal Against Death Sentence

DRAMATIC MOMENTS

Mrs. Hinks Collapses on Hear Husband's Fate

The headlines from the Bath Weekly Chronicle *after Hinks's appeal was dismissed.*

the following morning, with a crowd of around 500 waiting outside the prison, Reginald Hinks was executed. Connie Hinks said, 'I shall never believe he killed my father.'

Unfortunately, everybody else did.

8

THE LEMONADE BOTTLE MURDER OF HORFIELD

'It was a mad impulse.'

Is there a moment – however transitory – when a mild, inoffensive person can turn into a calculating, cold-blooded killer? Is there a particular mental and emotional 'trigger' that, once pulled, can start a chain of terrible events, seemingly unstoppable?

In a neat suburban street in the district of Horfield, towards midnight, Number 1 Hughenden Road was a hive of activity, lights blazing out into the late rainy September night. The year is 1950 and on this 20th day of the month, Mrs Ethel Worth, a 65-year-old widow, is leaving her home of 40 years, as a murder victim. Startled neighbours, peering past chintz curtains, are aghast at the shadowy scene. Two police constables, with the aid of torches and police car headlights illuminating the driving rain, are seen carrying a coffin to a small van and driving away at speed.

Fingerprint experts and photographers are busy inside Ethel Worth's cosy home whilst policemen guard the comings and goings of assorted investigators, as well as some reporters from the *Western Daily Press & Bristol Mirror*. The reporters' persistence is grudgingly rewarded when the Head of Bristol CID, Superintendent Melbourne Phillips, tells them: 'It is impossible at this stage to say whether or not there was foul play.'

Carefully chosen words from a seasoned police officer. Of course there was foul play – distressing and gratuitous foul play by a person or persons unknown. Superintendent Phillips wanted to gather his facts away from the gaze of the popular press, so that he could catch what he knew was a dangerous person. It was unlikely to be more than one intruder as the house had not been ransacked. There seemed to be no evidence of robbery or damage anywhere; just the slaying of a frail, elderly lady as a neighbour described her. It seemed that whoever killed Mrs Worth was let into the house as there was no sign of forced entry. Did Ethel Worth know her killer?

By the next morning the newspapers had managed to garner some additional information, as evidenced by the front page of the *Western Daily Press & Bristol Mirror* of Thursday 21st September:

HORFIELD WIDOW FOUND DEAD
HEAD WOUNDS
CID CALLED

The discovery of a 65-year-old widow dead in a chair at her home at 1 Hughenden Road, Horfield was being investigated by Bristol CID last night. The woman, understood to have head wounds, was Mrs Ethel Merinda Worth, who had lived in her secluded house in the quiet residential district for over 40 years.

The discovery was made by her son, 35-year-old Frederick Worth, worker at the BAC who lived with her.

On his arrival home last night, a sister, Mrs Sophia Billingham of 2 Church Road, Horfield, was called in by Mr Worth, prostrate after the discovery and too ill to talk.

Mrs Gertrude Waller of Gloucester Road, Bristol, another sister – the dead woman was one of 10 sons and daughters – said apparently Mrs Worth had been having her usual afternoon nap – she was lying in her chair dead, a glass of water at her side.

At this stage what the newspapers did not know was that Frederick Worth's obvious distress at finding his mother dead that night had been exacerbated by the way in which he made the discovery. Ethel Worth had appeared to be asleep in her chair by the sitting room fire. Her face had been covered with a reddish woolly coat, and when he lifted this away it revealed that she had been badly beaten about the head and neck. She had lost a lot of blood from a massive head wound. Frederick Worth, of course, was automatically a police suspect, having found the body, and because he was the only other person living in the house. It is not unknown for a family argument to get out of hand and for a child to kill a parent in a rage. Did Frederick kill his mother?

The police now worked hard in tracing anyone in the neighbourhood known to the murdered woman and her family. Frederick, like many people in this small community, was employed at the nearby Bristol Aircraft Company. The police decided that here was another source to check for possible visitors to Ethel Worth's house on that Wednesday.

The pathologist had now established that Mrs Worth died during the afternoon. She had been beaten about the head with a blunt instrument and then strangled. There was bruising to the front of her neck and a small bone in her throat was broken. Frederick had returned home for his lunch that Wednesday and then left his mother around 1.30 pm to return to work. A neighbour had seen Mrs Worth sitting and looking out the window at around 2 pm, and they had exchanged waves. This took Frederick out of the frame as it seemed clear that he had been at work when his mother was murdered. Frederick had confirmed that some money, a few pounds, had been taken from his mother's purse and that a watch was missing, as well as a pair of binoculars.

Further speculation was soon headed off, as the police made a remarkably swift arrest. By Friday 22nd September the front-page story had become:

LABOUR CHARGED WITH MURDER

A 49-year-old labourer Edward Woodfield, married, of 223 Southmead Road, Bristol, was last night charged with murdering Mrs Ethel Merinda Worth aged 64 who was

found dead in an armchair at her home in Hughenden
Road, Horfield, Bristol on Wednesday night.

Mrs Worth had head injuries. Woodfield will appear
before Bristol magistrates this morning.

This dramatic news ensured that, despite the persistent heavy
rain, queues began to form outside Bristol Magistrates' Court
for a chance to sit on the public benches and see what kind of
man would be charged with killing a defenceless elderly lady in
her own home.

This was to be the first of four magistrates' court remands for
Edward Woodfield, as the police forensic team and the Director
of Public Prosecutions made sure that they had all the evidence
they needed to secure a conviction.

Why Edward Woodfield? What was his connection with Ethel
Worth?

One person known to the family, and who used to visit Mrs
Worth, was Ted Woodfield, an ex-employee of BAC. In fact,
Frederick knew that his mother had lent Ted a pound or so to
tide him over whilst he tried to get his old job back. Frederick
was cross that his mother had done such a thing, since she had
only limited savings herself. Ted Woodfield had not been sacked,
but had left to try to get a better job. Having found it difficult
to find the sort of work he wanted, he was now trying to get his
old job back. Meanwhile he had signed on at the Labour
Exchange and his wife Catherine went out to work all day while
he hung around at home.

When he was questioned about his movements on the day
after the murder, the police officers asking the questions saw
immediately that Woodfield was uncomfortable speaking to
them. When told of Mrs Worth's murder, Woodfield said, 'Oh
I am sorry, this is the first I have heard about it.' Sergeant Cox
asked him to be very careful what he said about his movements
that Wednesday, adding 'Hughenden Road is a very short road
and if you did go there yesterday it may well be that somebody
saw you.'

Woodfield explained that he had been to the Labour Exchange
and then to an inn in Chock Lane, where he had two pints of

cider before returning home for some lunch. He then went to bed for a couple of hours. He then became distressed and agitated, put his head on his arms and started to cry. Sergeant Cox and Superintendent Phillips bided their time, and after a few minutes Woodfield looked up and said, 'It was a mad impulse.'

From this moment, the police knew they had their murderer. So, the question now turned to motive, but not only this. Even if stealing had been Ted Woodfield's motive, why murder a defenceless elderly lady?

His claim to have succumbed to 'a mad impulse' would now become the legal battle, rather than his guilt or innocence. But how convincing was this claim?

By the time Woodfield had finished his sworn statement to the police on that Thursday, they knew exactly what a terrible, cold-blooded and senseless murder had occurred. Now all they had to do was to produce all the forensic evidence in court to substantiate Woodfield's chilling confession. While the concerned neighbours had been gazing out at the frantic police activity that rainy Wednesday night, little could they have imagined on seeing Ethel Worth's coffin carried from the house what really had occurred, and how precarious life can be:

I signed on at the Exchange. While I was having my dinner, I thought I could get a couple of pounds out of poor Mrs Worth. My gaze fell on a lemonade bottle in the room and after dinner I put it in my pocket and went out. I went straight up to Mrs Worth's house, and knocked at the door. She came to the door and I put my hand into the inside breast pocket of my jacket. I think I pulled my wallet out a little – I wanted Mrs Worth to think I was going to pay her the pound I borrowed from her on Monday. She asked me to come in. As I followed her through the passage to the back room, I struck her on the head with the lemonade bottle. A mad impulse came over me to do it, I did not hit the old lady very hard, she went to the back room and sat in the chair. I hit her again with the bottle when she was in the chair. I don't think they were hard blows because I got frightened. She said, 'Don't, Ted.'

I was afraid if she came to, I should be caught, so I just squeezed her round the throat. I put on an old pair of gloves when I squeezed her.

I then took some money from the handbag in the cupboard in the room and went upstairs. I took a watch from a bedroom and I also took a pair of field glasses from the back room upstairs. I then left the house leaving the front door open and started to walk home.

At Horfield Common I threw the gloves and the bottle away.

I then went home and made a cup of tea. It was about 4.20 pm.

I then put the watch into a cigarette case and buried it with the field glasses just outside the back door. By then it was about 5 o'clock, and I got tea ready for my wife, she goes out to work. Later that night I felt I had to get rid of the money – I took my wife to the Beehive and bought her some drinks, I could not stay in, I thought the police would be coming for me, I spent an awful night.

The misplaced perceptions of what he was doing are chilling. Woodfield gives the vague impression that he's come to pay back the money Ethel Worth had kindly lent him. She invites him in. He hits her from behind with a weapon he had chosen to take with him. 'I did not hit her very hard' is added, as if this somehow mitigates the act of horror he was committing. Again, 'I don't think they were hard blows.' Ethel Worth pleads with him, but he ignores her and has the presence of mind to put on some gloves before he strangles her. Is this a mad impulse? He covers her face with her woolly coat and takes money and possessions – there is no awaking from a mad moment here, no remorse. In fact, he later takes his wife out to the pub spending the stolen money on drinks. The police were appalled at Woodfield's story.

This confession was guaranteed to secure his inevitable murder trial and likely execution, but crucial to a successful prosecution was evidence to substantiate his admission of guilt. The detectives were now able to set off to locate the murder weapon and the stolen goods.

Superintendent Phillips found the bloodstained gloves amongst the undergrowth in a disused allotment, whilst concealed under some rubbish in Woodfield's back garden was a cigarette case containing a gold watch, and hidden alongside this were the stolen binoculars. Meanwhile Detective Inspector Jesse Pane scoured Horfield Common and found a lemonade bottle smeared with blood that had been cast into the hedgerow.

On being shown the bottle, Woodfield said 'That's the one'. By this time Professor J.M. Webster, a Home Office pathologist, had been able to confirm that death had been due to manual strangulation after head injuries from which Mrs Worth bled profusely.

A lemonade bottle similar to the one used in the murder.

On a weekly basis Woodfield would make his brief appearances in the dock for further remands until the final committal at Bristol Magistrates' Court on Wednesday 18th October, where he was charged with the murder of Ethel Worth, now almost a month before. He was sent for trial at Bristol Assizes.

The much-awaited trial began on Wednesday 22nd November, and it was clear from the outset that Woodfield's defence was going to be insanity. The defence barrister in this case, J.D. Casswell KC, was determined to build on the 'mad impulse' confession and attempt to find a means to persuade a jury who would be hearing his cold, frightful confession that it was not a sane Edward Woodfield that had visited Mrs Worth that afternoon. The sane Woodfield was a mild, inoffensive man, whilst the Woodfield who clubbed her from behind with a lemonade bottle whilst she struggled to her chair, and who put on gloves before strangling her whilst she pleaded with him to stop, was a different, temporarily insane, *alter ego*. After all, he was to tell the jury, Woodfield had only to ask Ethel Worth to lend him some money. She had done so before, and there was no reason to think she would not do so again. Ted Woodfield had had no reason to kill her.

Casswell's strategy was to attempt to prove, through the testimony of a medical expert, that not only did Woodfield have a history of family members with varying neurological illnesses, but also Ted Woodfield himself had been ill with a mid-brain blood clot only three years previously. He would also call to the stand Catherine Woodfield, who had been married to Ted Woodfield for nineteen years, to testify how out of character this murderous and violent behaviour was. 'He was the kindest man I have ever known, I have never known him to be violent,' she would testify. The key to Casswell's defence plan, therefore, was whether there had been some form of emotional trigger that was pulled that September day, sending a cold-blooded killer to Hughenden Road rather than the real Ted Woodfield. Casswell admitted in his memoirs, 'I racked my brains to find some coherent form of argument that could save this obviously sick man from the gallows.'

The whole of that first trial day was given over to Casswell's 'Guilty but Insane' defence argument. It was agreed between the defence and the prosecution that there was no need to prove **who** had committed the crime, but it was vital to prove **why** it had been committed. It was laid before the jury to decide between unexplained temporary insanity, and greed backed up by no respect for human life.

Casswell even persuaded Ethel Worth's son, Frederick, to admit that he had never known Woodfield to be violent. The facts that he produced in an attempt to persuade the jury that family medical history was relevant were that Woodfield's father's mother and sister had been admitted to Gloucester Asylum, that his father's brother had died from a clot on the brain, that his father had died from meningitis aged only 33 and that Woodfield's mother had suffered from delusions.

Casswell was then able to build on this family history of neurological difficulties using the discovery by a specialist in 1947 that Woodfield himself had a clot of blood in the mid-brain which, the specialist claimed, could cause abnormal and violent reactions 'to trivial upsets'. Casswell had reached his 'emotional trigger' moment.

He needed to present the jury with the key 'trivial upset' that turned Edward Woodfield into a murderer that Wednesday afternoon in September.

Casswell produced such an incident in questioning Catherine Woodfield. He asked her, 'Has he ever lost his temper with you?'

'No,' replied Mrs Woodfield, 'I cannot say he ever did. He hates the sight of blood and on one occasion when he had seen a road accident he would not eat anything at all.'

'Have you ever seen him do anything violent?'

'No, not never,' she responded.

Casswell then came to the critical part of his defence. He asked her, 'Do you remember what happened on the morning of the twentieth?'

'I was just going out,' she answered, 'when the post came. My husband took in a letter which was from the Bristol Aeroplane Company. He opened it and I read it over his shoulder.'

'What did he do with the letter?'

'He was very upset and rolled it into a ball and threw it across the room, I have never known him do that before.' Catherine Woodfield went on to recount that the letter from BAC explained to Ted that they could not re-employ him. She added that he thought it was because of the dermatitis from which he suffered quite badly. She went off to work but worried about him all day, even having an impulse to return – but she did not return home until her usual time that evening, when they went out to the pub.

Casswell asked her if she had noticed anything unusual about her husband when she got home and she said she did not. 'Was he just as normal?'

'Yes.'

'Next morning did you go to work again? Did he seem normal or different?'

'Just the same.'

'Has he ever discussed the incident with you at all?'

'No.'

When supported by his medical expert, Dr Gibson, it was

possible, claimed Casswell, that the trivial incident of the letter would make voluntary control of his emotions deficient. Deficient enough to turn Woodfield into a cold-blooded killer was Casswell's unstated but clear message to the jury.

For the prosecution, Mr Maude, however, directly contradicted much of this testimony, claiming Woodfield had known quite well what he was doing. 'You don't want to go round hunting for motives; sometimes people are murdered because a fellow wants money. This man was activated by greed and he planned the theft and murdered her.' Initially Dr Gibson had testified that, from his examination, it was not possible to say that Woodfield had definitely known, or definitely had not known, what he was about. He might have lost control from the time he followed Mrs Worth along the passage. In cross-examination Dr Gibson conceded that it was quite possible for a man to be insane at the time and there to be no evidence two months afterwards.

Casswell's argument was not one the jury was likely to support, with no evidence of insanity other than one alleged example that had resulted in the murder of a kindly, frail lady in her own sitting room.

Besides, the prosecution produced its own neurological expert, Dr Ralph Hodge, Consultant Psychiatrist to the Burden Neurological Institute, who testified that he had examined the accused about a month after the offence and had found no sign of insanity. Hodge had come to the conclusion that Woodfield had been fully aware of what he was doing on 20th September.

Casswell knew his defence was badly flawed by the emotional magnitude of what his client had done, and by the evidence of previous planning (taking the weapon and the gloves before setting off to Hughenden Road). Why should the jury believe Dr Gibson rather than Dr Hodge?

He was left clutching at straws, saying he was very unhappy, and that perhaps he, as well as the medical experts, were missing crucial information that could prove the possibility of this kind of momentary insanity. 'I cannot help thinking there are more things in heaven and earth than are dreamed of in their philosophy,' he said, rather bizarrely. But he had also said to the jury in his final speech that to claim 'this man had suddenly evolved a beastly, cunning plot, I say it is so foreign to his personality it must have been some abnormal impulse which caused it. It was something which had made him a vicious beast'.

Horfield prison.

The jury did not agree with him. Two hours and forty-five minutes after retiring they pronounced Edward Woodfield 'Guilty' of the murder of Ethel Merinda Worth. Woodfield was staring fixedly ahead at the lamp suspended by a chain over the judge's dais. Asked if he had anything to say why sentence should not be passed upon him he replied, 'Yes sir, God knows best.' Justice Devlin then pronounced the death sentence.

This was, incidentally, J.D. Casswell's very last murder case as a defence counsel – he did not stay for the sentence, leaving for London whilst the jury was still out. He knew his final client was destined for the gallows.

A festive Christmas edition of the *Bristol Observer*, for Saturday 16th December 1950, carried a small item tucked down at the bottom of its front page, almost apologetically positioned as if not to draw any more attention to it than necessary. It merely read:

WOODFIELD EXECUTED

Edward Isaac Woodfield, 49, who was sentenced to death at Bristol Assize on November 23rd for the murder of Mrs Ethel Merinda Worth, a 65-year-old Horfield widow, was executed at Horfield Prison on Thursday morning.

9

EVIL EYES: MURDER IN LOXTON

*'It is not Marie that is dead. It is the evil
that was in her.'*

It was a pleasant late summer's morning. Indeed, this first day
of September 1954 promised to be as fair as the August it
had just left behind. The picturesque village of Loxton,
dwarfed by the magnificence of Crook's Peak, gave this north
Somerset village a distinctly Swiss appearance much appreciated
by the summer tourists on their trips out from nearby Weston-
super-Mare.

Mrs Eva Simmonds had set off from Garage Cottage to walk
the short distance to Gardeen, where she worked as a part-time
housekeeper. It was just after 8 am on this Wednesday and, as
Mrs Simmonds approached the large, detached, limestone house,
something did not seem quite right. When she got closer she saw
that the curtains in one of the bedrooms and the nearby upstairs
landing were still drawn. The bedroom was that of Miss Marie
Buls, an elderly lady who had recently had the misfortune to
have suffered a mild stroke, as well as broken her leg. Her
companion, Noreen O'Connor, however, was fit, active and an
early riser and always had the landing and bedroom curtains
drawn by the time Eva Simmonds arrived at 8.15 am to start
breakfast. Something was definitely wrong. Heaven forbid Miss
Buls had had another stroke, she thought.

Only yesterday she had been up and in good spirits when Eva
had taken her evening meal up to the bedroom. Indeed, she had
wished the old lady a fond good night when she had cleared the

Gardeen as it was when Noreen O'Connor and Marie Buls lived there together. (By kind permission of the Weston & Somerset Mercury)

dishes away around 7.30 pm, before leaving for the night. What on earth had happened? Eva Simmonds let herself in by the back door, straight into the kitchen, and began preparing the breakfast trays for both Marie Buls and Noreen O'Connor. At this moment Miss O'Connor walked in, looking pale and drawn and still wearing her dressing gown. Normally she would have been dressed and lively, sometimes far too lively first thing in the morning for Mrs Simmonds's taste, but she was a good employer and a kindly soul having taken Marie Buls under her wing, so to speak, after Marie had become too ill to look after herself. As Eva Simmonds looked up, Noreen O'Connor spoke slowly and a little shakily. She said: 'Something terrible has happened to Marie.'

Mrs Simmonds asked what Miss O'Connor meant, suspecting that she had been right about the meaning of the drawn curtains, and that Miss Buls had suffered another stroke. Noreen O'Connor did not answer and, instead, explained how she had been awake all night and she would have breakfast in her room. Mrs Simmonds took up her breakfast tray and, although it was not discussed, felt it was not appropriate to prepare a tray for Marie Buls unless asked to do so.

Unknown to the housekeeper, Noreen O'Connor was waiting for a visitor. At approximately 7.20 that morning, she had telephoned Peter Tiarks, whose family had employed Marie Buls for many years as a lady's maid to his late mother, to ask him to come at once and that 'something dreadful had happened'. Mr Tiarks had asked her what on earth she meant, and said that it would be difficult for him to come all the way from Dorset as he had a business appointment in Wales that day, but Noreen O'Connor had told him that it could not be spoken about on the telephone and that he must drive to Loxton immediately. She said that something terrible had happened to Marie and that she had been possessed of some evil. It was such a strange and dramatic call.

Marie Buls, now 77 years old, had been a dear and faithful companion to Peter Tiarks' mother for many years. Noreen O'Connor, similarly, had been a major strength as a companion and nurse to his late father and was now kindly nursing Miss Buls in turn, purely as an act of close friendship. Here were two very special women inextricably linked to his family, as if they were themselves blood relatives, and now something seemed to be very wrong. Miss O'Connor, aged 46, was not someone prone to panic, so without further hesitation Peter Tiarks set off in some anxiety from his home in Dorset to the small Somerset village of his childhood.

It was around 10 o'clock that morning when Eva Simmonds let Peter Tiarks into the house and showed him straight to the sitting room where Noreen O'Connor was lying on a sofa. On entering the room he immediately asked her what had happened. Her reply threw him.

'Surely you know?' she replied. He assumed by this, like Eva Simmonds, that Marie had suffered another stroke. Within a few brief sentences Peter Tiarks soon realised that Noreen O'Connor was not herself – she was almost trance-like in manner and her conversation rambled wildly. She went on to explain that, whilst she had been sitting and talking to Marie, she had seen evil in her old friend's eyes. This was not evident all the time; but when Marie had looked towards the corner of her room, the evil look appeared. At first, Noreen explained, she tried to avoid catching sight of this terrible gaze but it became stronger and suddenly she said there was one moment when the evil in Marie's eyes became so powerful, so strong, that 'I plucked them out'.

Peter Tiarks, shocked by this outburst and not wanting to believe what he had just heard asked her: 'Do you mean to say you plucked out Marie's eyes and she is now dead?'

In a frighteningly calm and reassuring way Noreen O'Connor replied, 'I plucked out Marie's eyes but it is not Marie that is dead. It is the evil that was in her.'

While Peter Tiarks struggled to take in what had just been said, a long rambling explanation came tumbling out as she tried to explain how she had expected him to visit her the previous night (although he knew no such arrangement had been made), that the evil influences had begun whilst she was listening to the wireless, and there had been noises upstairs with doors opening and shutting. She had had to go up and look after Marie, to try to remove these evil influences. She had sat holding Marie's hand for some considerable time, praying very hard to protect her from evil. Something had happened to Marie's eyes and she had slipped down to the floor.

Peter asked more directly if she had killed Marie, and Noreen replied, 'Well, I suppose she is dead but I did not kill her.'

Whilst Noreen O'Connor's distress and explanations continued, Peter Tiarks telephoned Dr Norman Cooper, who lived nearby at Winscombe. Dr Cooper set off immediately for Loxton, arriving at Gardeen by 11.30 am, and was immediately directed upstairs to Marie Buls's darkened bedroom. What he found was a distressing and terrible sight.

Miss Buls was lying on her back on the bedroom floor. She was dressed and her head was turned to the side facing a radiator, so her face could not clearly be seen. Her arms were folded, but her hands were frozen in a clutching motion as if trying to fend off an attacker. Her right hand was very bruised and swollen. Dr Cooper drew back the curtains and the morning light revealed a horrific sight that not even an experienced doctor could take in his stride. Marie's eyeballs had collapsed into their eye sockets. Her eyelids were torn and her eye sockets had been gouged clean of the living tissue.

As if this was not distressing enough, Marie's top lip had been torn back as far as the gum and it was clear that a tooth had been knocked clean from her mouth. Her right nostril was also ripped back as if something or someone using a claw-like grip had tried to tear it away from her face. He noticed small bruises on her right shoulder, where someone had possibly gripped hard to gain as much purchase as possible as they clawed viciously at her face. Blood was splattered on the floor and up the wall. Dr Cooper estimated that the poor woman had been dead for between seven and ten hours. Clearly something quite monstrous had happened in the early hours of that September morning, and Noreen O'Connor possibly held the key to these terrible events.

Whilst Dr Cooper had been upstairs dealing with this tragic scene, Noreen O'Connor had continued her rambling and somewhat incoherent conversation with an increasingly concerned Peter Tiarks. She had told him that there were words coming from Marie's mouth but they were not in Marie's voice. She had also made the bizarre claim that she had taken grass cuttings from Marie's eyes. Tiarks had told her that this was mad talk, to which her simple reply had been: 'I suppose so, but you don't think it mad do you? Surely the evil had to be got rid of?' Peter Tiarks had fallen silent, since there was no point in answering such a question. Noreen O'Connor, long-time family friend, companion and nurse to his late father, was no longer there; she had been replaced by someone he simply did not know.

A solemn Dr Cooper joined them and immediately told Noreen O'Connor he would have to ask her some questions about what he had found, and then he would have to inform the police. She told him that Miss Buls had looked odd, so rather than go to bed, she had gone into Marie's bedroom to sit with her, keep her company and hold her hand. She then explained how she had felt electric shocks coming from the bedspread so got up to leave the room, but when she touched the door, had felt the same shocks. This was a sign that Marie was in danger, so she had gone back to her friend's bedside to continue sitting with her and holding her hands. At this point a strange look had come into Marie's eyes and O'Connor also heard some voices. She told the doctor how she had squeezed Marie's hand and prayed very hard, but a voice had said to her 'this is my hate', and then Miss Buls had not been herself anymore. She now had evil in her.

Noreen O'Connor had not been able to avert her gaze from the evil that had appeared in Marie's eyes, and had decided that they must be removed. She told the doctor that she remembered no more until it was daylight. The evil spirits had disappeared, so she telephoned Peter Tiarks.

Like Peter Tiarks, Dr Cooper asked her if she knew what she had done and what the consequences of her actions had been. She told the doctor she did not feel she had done anything awful, but had got rid of something that was evil. The doctor now hesitated to ring the police, since keeping such a terrible tragedy confidential in such a small community would not be possible. The local telephone operator, necessary at that time since calls to the police had to be put through manually, would be able to listen to the conversation. It would be an unusual soul that would be able to keep a story like this secret for long. He left Miss O'Connor under Peter Tiarks' care and drove to Weston-super-Mare police station.

Detective Inspector Long arrived post-haste to inspect the scene prior to the body's removal. It took very little time for the Inspector to view the tragic scene and to tell Noreen O'Connor that he intended to detain her in connection with the death of Marie Buls. By this time, the village was buzzing with gossip as police cars arrived followed by an ambulance, and shortly after locals saw Miss O'Connor being shown into the back of a police car – the villagers were positively bursting with curiosity as to what on earth had been going on in their peaceful community. No doubt Eva Simmonds would have been under immense pressure to reveal what she knew, since her housekeeping position at Gardeen had now been dramatically terminated.

Gardeen today.

However, it would not be long before they would all be reading about this extraordinary case in their local paper, and be queuing up to attend the inquest and subsequent court proceedings.

Noreen O'Connor was taken to Weston-super-Mare police station. Her previous rambling conversations with Peter Tiarks and Dr Cooper had turned into the repeating of religious phrases and sayings. When Inspector Long told her he was arresting her for the murder of Marie Buls, she replied, 'I do not wish to say anything until I have seen my solicitor.' At the police station, in the presence of her solicitor, he formally charged her with the murder of Miss Buls, at which point she announced, 'I have no objection at all to telling them what happened and why it happened.' She then proceeded to become quite agitated, moving furniture about, singing, repeating the Litany and kneeling to pray, becoming quite violent when asked to accompany an officer to the cells. She continued in this vein for several hours.

Eventually, she was carried to the police cells shouting out prayers and religious phrases at the top of her voice.

Meanwhile, at Gardeen that same afternoon, Police Sergeant Christopher Woodriffe from Axbridge police station had arrived to make a careful search of Marie Buls's bedroom. He found a tooth, some loose hair and a broken comb of the sort worn in the hair. He also took a sample of blood from the floor. From the bathroom he gathered a dress, a brassiere, underslip and towel for examination at the Forensic Science Laboratory at Bristol. All that remained for additional forensic work was to take scrapings from under Noreen O'Connor's fingernails. If indeed she had clawed out Miss Buls's eyes, as confessed, crucial residual tissue samples would be found there. This was undertaken at 10.15 the next morning by Dr Arthur Rowley, the police doctor for Weston-super-Mare station, prior to O'Connor's appearance at Axbridge Magistrates' Court later that morning.

When a neatly dressed and extremely calm Noreen O'Connor was led into the magistrates' court, local reporters immediately began scribbling details of her loose-fitting grey coat, turquoise dress with matching beret, and noting how she sat quietly in the dock, hands folded in her lap. This surely was not a murderess, they thought. The hearing was very brief indeed. Detective Inspector Long outlined the charge, R.L. Gosling, who was appearing for Miss O'Connor, had no questions and there was no application for bail. She was remanded for another hearing to take place on the following Thursday, 9th September. Her plea was one of 'Not Guilty'.

As Noreen O'Connor left the court, she paused briefly by the door to smile at neighbours and gave a very slight bow before being taken back to the police cells. Before her journey to Exeter Prison, she was allowed, at her own request, to attend the opening of the inquest on Marie Buls that same afternoon. Dr Cooper confirmed the identity of the victim whilst Dr Rowley, who had conducted the post mortem, reported death was due to violent injuries to the eyes and face which had caused severe shock leading to death. He also added that he did not consider that these injuries were self-inflicted, a possibility he was obliged to consider. On hearing that a murder charge had been laid that very morning against Miss O'Connor the coroner, H.A. Horner, adjourned the inquest for eight weeks.

Local newspapers were falling over themselves to report this sensational tragedy. Was it really a murder, or could it have been a tragic accident? If murder, why on earth would Noreen O'Connor be charged with such a terrible crime? What possible motive could she have had? Miss O'Connor had been at the centre of village life. Whether it was fund raising for the church, supporting the local hunt, village fete or cricket team, she had been on hand to lend her support and often to present awards to village and neighbourhood achievers. Having spent a long time working for the much admired Frank Tiarks, Peter's father and head of one of the most influential local families, her village and community credentials were immaculate. This was indeed an incredible local story.

The *Weston Mercury & Somerset Herald* worked frantically to get their Friday 3rd September edition packed with verbal imagery. Also, they were able to steal a march over many rival papers which had a Thursday publication and were bemoaning the fact that they would be running a full week behind the events as they unfolded. They ran with the headline:

MURDER CHARGE FOLLOWS DEATH
OF AGED LOXTON WOMAN

They were able to put out three columns, including a picture of Noreen O'Connor and one of Gardeen, and to provide a long and detailed backdrop to what they knew was an extraordinary story whatever the final details would turn out to be. At this stage, of course, they knew nothing about O'Connor's claims that some kind of evil had possessed her elderly companion. The drama of that story was yet to come.

As far as Noreen O'Connor was concerned, the paper went on to describe her as a former staff nurse at The London Clinic and then continued:

Mr Tiarks' blonde companion-chauffeuse was a familiar figure at cricket matches, horse shows and similar events

Noreen O'Connor (3rd from right) at the East Brent Fete, just ten days before she murdered Miss Buls – this was her Lady Bountiful image. (By kind permission of the Weston & Somerset Mercury*)*

in which he continued, although an invalid, to take a great interest. She was 'My Lady Bountiful' in the Loxton district where she showed a special interest in the church – only a week or two ago she was one of the prime movers in organising a garden fete to raise funds for St Andrew's and the extension of the village hall and commercial affairs in general.

Extensive details were then provided of Frank Tiarks' considerable wealth, his role as a director of the Bank of England as well as a partner in a firm of merchant bankers, plus many other commercial activities. His death had occurred only two years previously and there was much local speculation that Noreen O'Connor had benefited considerably under his will. Indeed, Miss O'Connor had been left a trust fund and a directorship of the local Callow Rock Lime Company Ltd. What now needed explanation was the story behind these two spinsters living together at Gardeen, and how one came to be charged with the murder of the other.

In 1899 Marie Buls had come to Peter Tiarks' family home, North Lodge, Loxton from Micklenburg in Germany to work as a lady's maid to his mother Emmy Tiarks. In 1940, 63-year-old Miss Buls had been swept up in the United Kingdom's enemy alien internment policy which, in the early days of the Second World War, saw the British rounding up and interning both German and Austrian 'friendly aliens' beginning with those residing in the countryside. Instructions had been issued in July 1940 for the internment of female aliens, as well as those who were naturalised subjects of enemy origin. This was a tremendous emotional break with the family, who in turn pledged a home at North Lodge for Marie as soon as she was allowed back. Her successor in 1940 had been 32-year-old trained nurse Noreen O'Conner, who continued to care for Mrs Tiarks until she died in 1943, before being able to see Miss Buls again. Miss O'Connor then took up the position of nurse to Frank Tiarks with great local success, as the *Weston Mercury* had described.

She had gratefully received his gift of the house Gardeen in 1945, which meant she would have a permanent home of her own in the village. When in April 1952, after the death of Frank Tiarks, she had offered to share her home with Marie Buls, then 75, and to care for her in her senior years this action could only be admired. Now that same 'Lady Bountiful' was in Exeter Prison charged with Miss Buls's murder. So what had gone so wildly wrong?

Tuesday 7th September saw the funeral of Marie Buls. His mind reeling at the recent events, Peter Tiarks respectfully followed the brass-trimmed elm coffin, which was draped with a large cross of white dahlias and carried a centrepiece of pink carnations with red and pink roses. A card was inscribed 'Marie – From all the Family'.

Noreen O'Connor was to appear before Axbridge Magistrates' Court three times, flanked by a prison wardress and nurse. Each time she would confirm her identity with a simple 'Yes' and within minutes would be remanded again, still awaiting the decision of the Director of Public Prosecutions about when and how to proceed. Each time she appeared, more and more villagers would struggle to see her smartly dressed, calm façade, hoping to learn what had really happened. She in turn would acknowledge them with a faint smile.

It was only at her fourth Axbridge appearance on Friday 24th September that at last the public, and to their relief the local newspapers, learned details of the story. Reporters got more than they bargained for with headlines proclaiming:

NURSE ACCUSED OF MURDER
DRAMATIC STORY OF
'EVIL EYES'

As expected the public benches were crowded and Noreen O'Connor, again dressed in her grey coat with her now familiar mauve beret, smiled and listened intently to everything being said. Phillip Radcliffe, for the Director of Public Prosecutions, explained the background to Miss Buls's position in the Tiarks family and her inability to stay in that position during the war when interned; to how Miss O'Connor took over her role in 1940; arriving at the crucial and kindly relationship shared by the two spinsters living together at Gardeen that ended so tragically on 1st September 1954. All the strange occurrences of that fateful day came tumbling out to a hushed courtroom as Peter Tiarks and Dr Cooper recounted their conversations with Noreen O'Connor and her confessions. Peter Tiarks also recalled that she spoke about listening to the radio before going up to sit with Marie Buls. She had explained that she had been listening to news about a possible German rearmament and 'all those evil things'. It was after hearing that news item that she had heard the opening and shutting of doors upstairs, felt concerned about Marie Buls's welfare, and so gone to her.

The rest of the tragic events and the horrific detail of Marie Buls's injuries and death were outlined. Dr Rowley explained how he had found loose hair clutched in the right hand of the deceased. The hand had been swollen and covered in blood and the face had also been covered in blood. The eyes had been ruptured and in his opinion this had been caused by pressure.

There was little that Herrick Collins, representing Noreen

THE WESTON MERCU

Court Told That Woman On Murder Charge Spoke Of "Evil Look"

WITNESS SAYS SHE TOLD HIM: "I PLUCKED OUT MARIE'S EYES"

ACCUSED SENT FOR TRIAL AT SOMERSET ASSIZE

A 46-year-old former nurse, accused of murdering an elderly German woman, formerly a lady's maid, was alleged by a witness, at Axbridge magistrates' court to have told him that she had plucked out the woman's eyes after seeing an "evil

"G

The headline in the Weston Mercury & Somerset Herald. *(By kind permission of the* Weston & Somerset Mercury)

O'Connor, could do apart from laying down small areas of doubt, clarifying seemingly small details and probing the witnesses' accuracy of recall. But he did it superbly. He questioned Dr Cooper about the possibility that Miss Buls perhaps had died from a stroke prior to the attack to her face. He pointed out that there had been no injuries apparent on his client and that, as Miss Buls already had suffered two strokes, a third stroke brought on by some form of emotional stress was a possibility. Dr Cooper agreed that this was a possibility. Collins also asked Dr Cooper whether the position of the body was 'consistent with that of a person who had fallen or slipped off the bed?'

'It could have been, yes,' replied Dr Cooper.

'Was her head also close on the other side to the radiator?' Collins asked.

'Yes,' replied Dr Cooper. Herrick Collins went on to clarify that there had been no blood found on the bed itself, and perhaps it was possible that Miss Buls had in fact died around twelve hours prior to his visit rather than the seven to ten hours he had claimed. Dr Cooper conceded this was within the range of possibility. Without saying as much Collins seemed to be exploring the possibility that, if Marie Buls had suffered a stroke, fallen from the bed, hit her head on the radiator and died prior to the attack on her face, his client could no longer be convicted of a murder charge.

He pursued the same theme with Dr Rowley, the pathologist, hoping to show that the substantial quantity of blood on the floor and walls could have come from a person who had already died from a stroke. Dr Rowley, however, thought that this would be unlikely, although he could not rule out the possibility of a stroke having occurred just prior to death. Collins also established that Sergeant Woodriffe, who had searched Miss Buls's bedroom that day had not found any form of blunt instrument that could have caused the bruising to the head outlined in the pathologist's report, providing more support for his 'falling out of bed' theory.

The magistrates, however, decided that there was enough evidence to commit Noreen O'Connor for trial at Wells Assizes on 15th October. She bowed her head and, looking at Magistrate Mrs Greenhill, said softly, 'Thank you, madam.' Herrick Collins added, 'On behalf of the accused, she says she is not guilty and reserves her defence.' This time, Noreen O'Connor was sent all the way to Holloway Prison to await her October trial.

The court at Wells was packed, as both local and national media had made much of the 'evil eyes' story and the gruesome details that telling and retelling entailed. Is it possible that Noreen O'Connor had truly confronted an evil presence during that fateful night? Why would a person of such Christian fortitude suddenly become so obsessed with the idea of evil possessing Marie Buls and be driven to pluck out her friend's eyes?

The answers to these questions came from two very different sources. Firstly, however, Norman Skelhorn, QC, for the prosecution, made it clear that there was no possibility of the defence challenging the fact that it was Noreen O'Connor who had inflicted such terrible injuries on Miss Buls, and that she had died as a result of the shock induced by the injuries. The only explanation could be what he referred to as an 'insane attack'.

Then, a major clue that mental changes had occurred in Noreen O'Connor and which supported the idea of an 'insane attack', came, in fact, from one of the key defence witnesses, Maurice Bailey a former clerk of Axbridge Rural District Council. Now a director of Callow Rock Lime Company where Miss O'Connor was also a director, he had known her for six years and indicated that she was a diligent and efficient woman, always busy. However on 31st August 1954, when she came into the office, he had asked her about a recent business trip to Plymouth.

She had told him she had lunched at the same hotel and at the same table as she and Frank Tiarks had been accustomed to use when he was still alive and she used to drive him on such trips. Bailey testified: 'She told me that Mr Frank Tiarks was helping her and she felt he was always with her to guide her in what she did. She then said very dramatically, "All will be well but in a far different way than what you think."' She had then leaned over the desk and, uncharacteristically, gripped Bailey's hand, asking him: 'Have I been behaving queer lately? If I have, it will be different now because the evil spirit is dead forever.' Then very softly, she had added: 'You know Marie is ...?' She had not finished the sentence but stood up and turned towards the window with the comment 'If we trust in God, all will be well.' She had then spoken of being so very happy and, on a recent trip to Weston-super-Mare with Eva Simmonds and her daughter, insisting they both sung hymns with her to share her happiness. She had finished the encounter with Maurice Bailey by saying 'The fight is over, the evil is dead', and beginning to sing the first line of 'The Strife is O'er, the Battle Done'.

He had asked her, 'Shall I see you tomorrow?'

She had replied, 'I don't know where I will be tomorrow. I feel so happy I might be anywhere.'

He was asked by Skelhorn, 'Did you form any opinion about the state of her mind?'

'Yes,' testified Mr Bailey. 'I definitely came to the conclusion that she was mentally deranged.'

Noreen O'Connor. (By kind permission of the Weston & Somerset Mercury)

This was what the prosecution wanted to hear. They had expert medical witnesses who had made detailed assessments of Noreen O'Connor's mental state whilst in Holloway Prison and they were clear that the answers to her frenzied attack on Miss Buls lay in a 'disease of the mind'. Dr Desmond Curran, psychiatrist at St George's Hospital, London, was emphatic that O'Connor had not known what she was doing when she gouged out Marie Buls's eyes, other than trying to protect her. Her mental state was one of 'acute mania'.

Reminding the jury that there was no doubt that Noreen O'Connor was guilty of murder, Mr Justice Byrne said they must also take account of the fact she was suffering from defect of reasoning. She did not know that what she did was wrong. Without retiring, the jury returned a unanimous verdict of 'Guilty but Insane'.

Passive, pale but composed, Noreen O'Connor listened to the judge ordering her detention as a Broadmoor patient '... until Her Majesty's pleasure be known'. She bowed slightly to the judge and turned away for the nurse and wardress to lead her from the dock. She was now the patient not the nurse, and would remain so until her death 29 years later.

10

THE TERRIBLE DEEDS
OF JOHN STRAFFEN

'It only took a couple of minutes and she was dead.'

Murder is horrific. Taking away the lives of others is the ultimate theft and leaves such a complexity of emotional turmoil amongst family and friends that they too become victims. When the murdered are children with lives yet to live and when, exploiting their innocence, they are tricked into befriending their murderer, it adds such a depth of depravity and generates such tangible anger and anguish that it is difficult to imagine who could do such things.

John Straffen could and did.

Straffen holds the dubious distinction of being Britain's longest serving prisoner, being held not only for the terrible crimes he committed during the summer of 1951 in Bath, but also another carried out during the following spring in the area near Broadmoor where he was incarcerated. This is also a story of judicial and custodial incompetence. Alongside the horrible slaying of at least two young girls, in his 56th year of incarceration Straffen continues to pursue a legal challenge against his conviction for a third murder, although he admits to those that occurred in Bath in the fateful year of 1951. Fateful, that is, for Brenda Goddard and Cicely Batstone and their families.

In the countryside around Bath, the early 1950s were a time of children playing in the streets, woodland adventures and, if you were lucky enough to have some pocket money, going unaccompanied to the afternoon pictures or the local sweetshop – hopefully both! Adults were around but at a comfortable distance, summer play was just that and the only rules were to keep out of trouble, don't tear your clothes and be back in time for tea. This now seems a world apart, the rules changed beyond recognition, rigidly drafted to keep such precious lives within sight or within tight home boundaries. Even within the confines of the home, a battle now rages to prevent innocence being tainted and taken by 'electronic virtual strangers' enticing and beckoning – tempting young adventurers out of the 'chat room' to meet with them face to face.

It was in this 1950s lost world of innocent play that six-year-old Brenda Goddard came face to face with her stranger, 21-year-old John Straffen from Bathampton. The date was Sunday 15th July and, playing on Rough Hill close to her Bath home in Camden Crescent, Brenda was happily picking wild flowers when she heard a tall, pale stranger greeting her and telling her that higher up the hill there were many more flowers for her to pick. Trusting his advice, she gladly went with him to do just that, even allowing Straffen to help her over a small fence into a wooded copse. Once in the copse, he strangled her, then spent the rest of the afternoon at the cinema eating sweets and watching a film called *Shockproof*. Later he was to say it was to give the police, 'something really to do'.

John Straffen had built up a history with the police authorities after coming to Bath with his family in 1938. Put on probation for stealing, he was sent to a special school for breaching his probation. By 1947, as a 17-year-old youth, he was accused of assaulting a 13-year-old girl at Bathwick. He was reported to have placed his hand over her mouth, saying, 'What would you do if I killed you? I have done it before.' However, no action was taken against Straffen for this serious assault. Other charges of theft followed, including an episode in which he wrung the necks of five chickens belonging to the father of a girl he was angry with. Remanded to Horfield Prison, he admitted to over a dozen housebreaking offences for which he was not under suspicion, which led to a medical examination of his condition. The Medical Officer to Horfield Prison certified him as 'feeble-minded' (in the terminology of the day) and he was sent to a special facility at Almondsbury, called Hortham Colony, which is situated to the north of Bristol.

Hortham Colony was an open, not a secure facility and John Straffen was classified as 'not of violent or dangerous propensities'. Absconding several times, he was eventually released on licence, first in July 1949 to an agricultural hostel at Winchester, but a stealing offence returned him to Hortham. Once back there he settled down enough to be given leave on a special licence in February 1951, taking a job with a market gardener in Bath.

Only five days before Straffen met and murdered Brenda Goddard, he had been examined at Bristol hospital. Tests revealed 'wide and severe damage to the cerebral cortex'. This was thought to be as a result of contracting encephalitis as a toddler, whilst living in India when his father was in the armed forces. Despite these findings, Straffen's release on licence was renewed by the doctor and by 15th July Brenda Goddard was dead, almost, it seemed, as a revenge attack against the authorities who, he considered, bothered him on trivial grounds.

The agony of that terrible Sunday afternoon in Bath had begun when Brenda, who had only gone outside around 2 pm, failed to come back indoors to get ready for Sunday School. She was being looked after by Mr and Mrs Pullen whilst her widowed mother was working. Brenda was reported missing by a distraught Mrs Pullen about 3.15 pm and the police discovered her body at 7.10 that evening. This innocent young girl had not only been strangled but also viciously struck on the head with a stone.

The newspapers carried a description of a tall man in a blue suit, aged about 35, who had been seen by Mrs Pullen near to the house when she went out to call Brenda in to get ready. Police interviews of suspects eventually reached John Straffen at the end of July. He admitted to having been in the woods on the afternoon of the murder and had read the newspaper report concerning the hunt for a man aged around 35 but said '... as I am only 21, I did not think it referred to me'. He denied he had abducted and murdered Brenda Goddard.

Straffen was not arrested as there was a lack of evidence against him, but a few days after his questioning on 31st July, he

John Straffen is arrested.

was interviewed again and made a second statement to the police. However, he remained a free man whilst the police continued to seek evidence of Brenda's killer. On 9th August, Straffen went to the Forum Cinema in Bath to see *Tarzan and the Jungle Queen*. Also enjoying that film was nine-year-old Cicely Batstone. Straffen befriended Cicely and told her about another film he was going to see across town at the Scala Cinema, *She Wore a Yellow Ribbon*. He persuaded her to come with him on the short bus ride. Cicely never got as far as the bus stop. Straffen took her to Tumps Field and cold-bloodedly strangled her.

Police were delayed in beginning the search for Cicely as her parents had assumed she was with one of their other three children (aged 16, 19 and 21), so it was not until 11 o'clock that night that the panic really began. Meanwhile, John Straffen had called by the local chip shop for sixpenny-worth, strolled home and spent a peaceful night, appearing puzzled when the police called round at 9 o'clock the following morning to question him. They were not misled by false identifications this time, but had received evidence from a witness who knew who Straffen was and had seen him with Cicely. Straffen had also been seen by a courting couple taking the young girl into Tumps Field, and a passing policeman's wife later saw him in the same field and was able to tell the police where it was likely the body had been left.

'Is it about the little girl I was at the pictures with last night?' Straffen inquired of the police. 'She was dead under the hedge when I left her.'

Clearly the police had the murderer and within that same afternoon John Straffen is reported to have said to a police sergeant: 'Can I speak with you? I want to show you how I did in the first girl.'

After describing how he had strangled Brenda Goddard, he added, 'She never screamed at me when I squeezed her neck, so I bashed her head against the wall. I didn't feel sorry and forgot about it.' He told another officer, 'It only took a couple of minutes and she was dead.'

His trial was set for 17th October 1951 at Taunton Assizes. A strong medical defence was mounted to 'prove' he was not fit to plead. Not only was it claimed that he did not understand what 'guilty' meant, but also that he did not understand the trial process and what was going on, either in his defence, or in the prosecution against him. The concluding remarks to this application to the court not to go ahead with the trial are now part of key legal precedent. The judge, Mr Justice Oliver, ruled:

> Members of the jury, in this country we do not try people who are insane, so insane as not to understand what is going on; you might as well try a babe in arms. If the man cannot understand through insanity what is going on and is unable to tell his counsel what his defence is, we do not try him. Will you return the verdict that he is insane so as to be unfit to plead, and then I can deal with him?

The jury duly obliged and Justice Oliver committed him to Broadmoor with the words: 'He will be detained in safe custody during His Majesty's pleasure.'

Six months later, on 29th April 1952, John Straffen climbed

out of Broadmoor unchallenged. Left to sweep a yard next to an unlocked security gate, he walked through the gate, clambered onto the roof of a small storage shed with the help of an oil drum, dropped down outside the hospital perimeter and strolled off. This was not a spontaneous escape as he had managed to sneak back his civilian clothes, which he wore in readiness under the distinctive Broadmoor work clothes.

On escaping, Straffen made his way through the Berkshire countryside, even calling at a house to ask for a glass of water which the lady of the house willingly supplied. Setting off again through woodland, he emerged at Farley Hill and was given another glass of water by a children's nurse working at a large house nearby. During his escape John Straffen was seen by several more people in the village, and in particular was seen standing near the school and close by was a little girl on her bicycle. Straffen was even invited into Farley Hill House for a cup of tea. After a rather bizarre conversation with the lady of the house, about Broadmoor and whether patients escaped and whether the attendants search for them or not, and what the six o'clock news might report that evening, he headed off in the general direction of Wokingham.

There were subsequent reports that the Broadmoor authorities, together with the police, had flung a massive net across the country to snare Straffen, but the country-wide search seems, in practical terms, to have consisted of two Broadmoor nurses on push bikes.

Straffen, meanwhile, managed to get a lift to a bus stop a few miles along the road to Wokingham. As he was dropped off, he noticed uniformed Broadmoor staff and ran behind a nearby pub, but Mrs Miles (who had given Straffen his lift) pointed him out. Struggling violently, he was recaptured after four hours of liberty and taken for questioning while another drama was unfolding close by.

It was discovered that five-year-old Linda Bowyer, out for a bicycle ride, had disappeared. When her body was found in a dell of spring bluebells, she had been strangled, just like Brenda Goddard and Cicely Batstone. However, before even being questioned about the tragic discovery of Linda Bowyer, Straffen is reported to have said, 'I know what you policeman are. I know I killed two little children, but I did not kill the little girl with the bicycle.'

The newspapers were in no doubt about two issues: that Straffen had murdered for the third time, and that Broadmoor security was a bad joke and a threat to the local community. It was learned that the hospital had no alarm sirens to alert local residents when an escape occurred. Rather then send Straffen back to Broadmoor, at least at this sensitive stage, he was remanded to the hospital wing at Brixton Prison.

For residents of Bath, emotions ran high. Another little girl had been murdered in the same manner. Would Cicely Batstone and Brenda Goddard at last find the justice that some felt they had been denied? Would John Straffen stand trial this time, and be forced to account for his actions?

It is this area of medico-legal wrangling that puts the John Straffen case into the annals of British legal history. Families and communities want to see justice, and especially want to see a serial killer stand trial, yet as Mr Justice Oliver ruled in the Bath murders the year before, '... you might as well try a babe in arms'.

Should Straffen still be seen in this light? What could possibly have changed in seven or eight months to justify putting him on trial for the murder of Berkshire's Linda Bowyer, but not Bath's Brenda Goddard and Cicely Batstone? Complicating the picture right from the moment of his committal to Reading magistrates on 15th May was the claim by Straffen's defence counsel that, apart from the 'fitness to plead' issue which Justice Oliver had raised, the time the murder was said to have occurred, between 5.45 pm and 6.15 pm, did not match Straffen's movements as he fled through Berkshire intent on returning to his home town of Bath. If John Straffen did not murder Linda Bowyer, then another child killer was on the loose. This possibility was something no one wanted to face.

Now, what had begun with the despicable murder of two young girls in Bath for which no adversarial trial had taken place was turned on its head as a further tragic murder in Berkshire was made the trigger for the prosecution to push Justice Oliver's ruling to one side. The trial that began in Winchester on 21st July 1952 before Mr Justice Cassels was to make legal history. Apart from anything else, the gladiatorial styles of the defence and prosecution would keep the national and local newspapers screaming with editorial partiality. Prosecuting with a determination to overcome Mr Justice Oliver's 'babe in arms' ruling was the Solicitor-General himself, Sir Reginald Manningham-Buller, QC. His nickname in court circles was, in fact, 'Bullying-Manner'. So important was the move to trial seen to be that the Director of Public Prosecutions also attended the court hearing that day. Appearing for Straffen's defence was a sharp, young, 'Old Bailey-experienced' prosecuting counsel, in this case taking on the mantle of defender, Henry Elam (later to become one of London's most senior criminal judges).

Manningham-Buller called three doctors to confirm that, despite a mental age of around nine-and-a-half, John Straffen's declared ability to understand four out of the Ten Commandments overruled Oliver's previous judgment and that he could understand what was happening and stand trial. In questioning Dr James Murdoch of Wandsworth Prison, one of the medical experts for the prosecution's case, Elam asked: 'In your view was he sane?'

'Yes,' answered Dr Murdoch.

'He is sane although he was in Broadmoor?' retorted Elam.

'Yes,' confirmed Dr Murdoch. 'There are quite a number of sane people in Broadmoor.' The tension in the courtroom was broken as laughter ensued.

The first round went to the prosecution, who won the right for the trial to proceed. John Straffen duly pleaded ' Not Guilty' to the charge of murdering Linda Bowyer. But now a major legal hurdle emerged – Straffen had admitted to the murders of Bath's Brenda Goddard and Cicely Batstone but he had never been charged with these murders. Was this declared guilt to be admissible, given that the trial was for murdering one little girl in Berkshire, not two little girls in Bath? A major tenet of British law is that a person's past convictions cannot be revealed to the jury until after it has reached its verdict.

Everybody knew that in fact this had to be Brenda and

Cicely's day in court as well as Linda's – the desire for justice to be seen to be done for their murders was overwhelming and palpable, and the national and local press were in full pursuit of this as the only acceptable outcome.

So it was held to be – the murders in Bath of Brenda Goddard and Cicely Batstone did not constitute past convictions, so they could form a very important platform for the prosecution's case given their 'striking similarities' to Linda Bowyer's murder. After all, if Straffen indeed was not guilty of this murder, then it needed to be known and the pursuit of the real murderer continued. Implicitly, however, everyone knew this was to be the trial that the press and public had been denied the previous year – a form of public justice that had not been possible at the time. One further hurdle to cross was the request by the prosecution to use Straffen's declaration to the police on his recapture that 'I didn't kill the little girl with the bicycle.'

How could he have known that a little girl on a bicycle had recently been murdered when it had not been revealed to him at that time? Elam, for the defence, maintained he could have been aware of newspaper coverage or perhaps been told or inferred it. The prosecution won this legal argument but then catastrophe struck and before the trial could begin in earnest it was abandoned. The trial could not go ahead, ruled the judge, because it had become known that one of the jurors had been arguing about the case in a public forum, namely the Southsea Liberal Club, and had clearly stated in front of other members that, having examined trial documents and maps of where the body was found and Straffen's movements that day, he was not guilty. Apparently the juror had rather bizarrely claimed that 'one of the witnesses was responsible for the murder'.

The trial was stopped and instead of replacing the aberrant juror, the whole process of empanelling a new jury began anew, much to the media's disgust. The newspapers had no doubts about who had murdered three innocent girls and provocatively featured pictures of their mothers sharing their mutual grief over tea. The fresh trial found John Straffen guilty of murder – a last emotional plea to the jury by his defence counsel had not worked. Elam had explained in his summing up why he had not called Straffen himself to give evidence in his own defence: 'The spectacle of a mental defective giving evidence would indeed be a pathetic, tragic sight and one I am not going to ask you to see.'

John Straffen was duly sentenced to death and held in the condemned cell at Wandsworth Prison in London awaiting execution on 4th September.

John Straffen later in life.

The storm clouds had always been very dark and brooding over the issue of someone declared insane and sent to Broadmoor and then, within months rather than years, declared sane and responsible for his actions. Now, the completed trial, the guilty verdict and the imminent prospect of executing someone, however despicable and evil, with a declared mental age of nine-and-a-half, saw these storm clouds burst and raging arguments bandied to and fro between doctors, psychiatrists, lawyers, liberals and conservatives, with the media providing sudden jagged lightning flashes in asserting that we must hang child killers.

The Home Secretary intervened and, on 29th August 1952, John Straffen was reprieved and his sentence commuted to life imprisonment. The storm has not stopped raging from that moment. Still in custody, Britain's longest-serving prisoner has always admitted murdering Cicely Batstone and Brenda Goddard but always denied murdering Linda Bowyer. From this he has never wavered and, given his limited mental abilities (say those who believe him), he could not have kept up this consistency for so long.

If Straffen did not murder Linda Bowyer as he murdered Brenda Goddard and Cicely Batstone – then who did?

11

COLD CASE MURDERS OF BRISTOL AND BATH

'There are people out there who are going to find us knocking on their doors in the future, we never forget.'

(Detective Sgt Gary Mason: Cold Case Team,
Avon and Somerset, 'Unearthing Evidence'
page 3 in *Police – The Voice of the Service*,
September 2004)

Put good old-fashioned police work in the mix with the new forensic possibilities of DNA evidence and computer technology and a variety of unsolved crimes going back many years are now being solved. Several police forces across the country have set up successful 'cold case teams', often bringing back into the force retired police officers who originally worked on the case and were frustrated at leaving it unsolved. This new impetus brings them satisfaction at finally reaching a conclusion and apprehending the perpetrators, not to mention the welcome relief to families, friends and victims alike who were left without seeing justice being done.

Avon and Somerset Police have a dedicated team, including previously retired CID officers, painstakingly picking up the threads of unsolved cases and using all that modern methods have to offer to get new results and close the cases. Described by the police as akin to archaeology: 'Evidence can be stored in different places, old witnesses need to be tracked down and a picture of the past needs to be recreated.' (*Police – The Voice of the Service*: September 2004, page 3)

The public, whose ability to pick up and pass on crucial information and clues is paramount, are still the most important ingredient in solving crimes; but as cases become colder and colder over the years, the prospect of someone coming forward with information leading to a conviction becomes less likely but still possible.

The tragic murder of elderly widow Helen Fleet in Westbury Woods, Weston in 1987, recounted below, remains in the cold case file, unfortunately, but somebody knows something and it is still possible to bring a murderer to justice. Two other unsolved murder cases also still open to the cold case team to solve are those of Beryl Culverwell, murdered at her Bath home in 1978, and Shelley Morgan, murdered in 1984 on a day out from Bedminster to the Avon Gorge. Both murders are still of major concern to Avon and Somerset's cold case team – are you able to assist them?

(I) MOTIVELESS MURDER IN WESTON

'Somebody must have seen something.'

(Superintendent Ray Sarginson, April 1987)

The local newspaper reports of the murders of teenagers Karen Hastings and Mandy Cottom were to grip and shock the people of the Weston area from September 1986 onwards. The full story is given in chapter 6. By the spring of 1987, when many of the shocking details of that case had been revealed but the trial was still to he held, another local headline battered a disbelieving local population.

BRUTAL KILLING OF WIDOW SHOCKS TOWN

The murder of 66-year-old Helen Fleet on Saturday 28th March 1987 was another vicious blow to the area, except this time there was no immediate, clear murder suspect, no obvious motive, just a stark, brutal killing as the headline proclaimed.

Brutal killing of widow shocks town

THE BRUTAL and apparently motiveless killing of a Weston-super-Mare widow has sent shock waves through the town. Frail Mrs Helen Fleet was viciously murdered in a frenzied attack as she walked her dogs in Worlebury Woods above Weston. A full-scale murder hunt is continuing, and police appealed yesterday for any information that might help identify the killer.

Mrs Fleet (66), who lived with her widowed sister in Osborne Road, was repeatedly stabbed, beaten about the head and then strangled near the water tower in the woods only yards from Worlebury Hill Road.

Her two bewildered dogs led a friend, Mrs Sylvia Lewis, of Lark

By Sally Challoner

Road, Mead Vale, to the body when she discovered them barking and running about on their own. Mrs Fleet was last seen alive at 10.45 am on Saturday. She dropped off her sister, Mrs Betty Brough, in Alexandra Parade.

Mrs Fleet had driven to the woods in her blue Datsun car. On

● A recent picture of Mrs Fleet out walking her dogs.

metal detectors, in a bid to find the murder weapon, and making house-to-house enquiries and vehicle checks. An incident room at the police station is linked to a mobile headquarters in the woods.

"This was a vicious and motiveless attack on a defenceless old lady," said Det Supt Ray Sarginson, who is leading the investigation. "Clearly the killer is a dangerous man who must be caught."

"We have had a good response from the public," he said. The incident room at Weston police station has handled almost 100 calls, but he appealed to anyone who saw or heard anything suspicious in the area between 11 am and 1 pm last Saturday to come forward.

"It is a very busy wood," he added. "Somebody must have seen something."

The murder weapon, believed to be a small knife, has not been found despite an intensive and painstaking search of the woods undergrowth and brambles. A knife dredged up from a nearby drain had been there for some

ing of an inquest on Mrs Fleet that cause of death was manual

The headline in the Weston Mercury, *3rd April 1987.*
(By kind permission of the Weston & Somerset Mercury)

Mrs Fleet lived with her 64-year-old sister, Mrs Betty Brough, also a widow. They had moved to the town only a few years before. Both sisters were friendly and known about town: Helen in particular would be seen regularly walking her dogs Bilbow and Cindy in the local woods, or in Ashcombe Park. She was last seen alive by her sister on that Saturday morning when they left home together in Mrs Fleet's car accompanied by the dogs. Betty was not a walker and, at 10.45 am, Helen dropped her sister off in Alexandra Parade to do some shopping whilst she drove on to Worlebury Hill Road to walk the dogs. She parked the car and set off for her usual walk in Worlebury Woods. It was some hours later, after Mrs Fleet had failed to return to pick up her sister, that a friend, Mrs Sylvia Lewis from nearby Lark Road, Meadvale, saw Cindy and Bilbow barking and running around on their own. She saw no sign of Helen Fleet. When the dogs ran back into the woods, the worried Mrs Lewis decided to follow them.

Sitting nearby was local bus driver Stuart Pink parked up in his Badger Line bus at the Worle Hill Terminus. He could see an anxious woman run out of the woods and then make a bee-line for a nearby house.

Mr Pink later said, 'I saw her go into the corner house, so when she came out with the couple, I asked her what was wrong. She thought at first her friend had just collapsed.' In fact, Helen Fleet had been repeatedly stabbed, beaten about the head, and then strangled. It was a sight that Stuart Pink, David and Hazel Davies (the couple in the house on the corner from whom Sylvia Lewis sought assistance) and Sylvia herself would never forget. Mr Pink exclaimed it would haunt him for the rest of his life.

Protected by her dogs, who would not allow any of them to get closer than ten feet or so, lay the body of the savagely murdered widow. Stuart Pink coaxed away Bilbow, a little highland terrier, then took off his Badger Line company tie and used it as a lead, while Sylvia Lewis took hold of Cindy, a brown mongrel – they were friendly dogs, just bewildered at what had happened to their owner. Stuart Pink later described what he saw: 'There was a bruising around her neck and I could see two bloodstains on her side,' he said. The police quickly arrived having been called by David and Hazel Davies and the site was sealed off as a crime scene. So overcome was Stuart, that a company bus inspector had to be called from the depot to drive his bus back there, since Stuart was far too upset to do so. 'It suddenly hit me what I had just seen,' he later told local reporters, 'and I just burst into tears, I was so shaken.' The search for forensic evidence and clues to the identity of the murderer, or perhaps murderers, had begun.

Sally Challoner, a local reporter for the *Weston Mercury, Somerset and Avon Herald*, captured the local mood exactly in her report for 3rd April in which she wrote:

The brutal and apparently motiveless killing of a Weston-super-Mare widow has sent shock waves through the

BRISTOL & BATH WHODUNNIT?

The police begin their search for evidence. (By kind permission of the Weston & Somerset Mercury)

town. Frail Mrs Helen Fleet was viciously murdered in a frenzied attack as she walked her dogs in Worlebury Woods above Weston. A full-scale murder hunt is continuing. The police appealed yesterday for any information that might help identify the killer.

So far, the police believed the murderer had struck at around 12.20 pm on that fatal Saturday. A couple walking in the woods reported hearing a single, piercing scream at that time. Detective Superintendent Ray Sarginson, who had taken charge of the investigation, set up a mobile headquarters in Worlebury Woods to keep as close as possible to the scene and any local witnesses who might come forward. He said, 'This was a vicious and motiveless attack on a defenceless old lady. Clearly the killer is a dangerous man and he must be caught ... it is a very busy wood, somebody must have seen something.'

This statement has all the ingredients of the worst nightmare. It is a murder of a defenceless elderly lady and, according to the police, without motive. The Home Office pathologist, Professor Bernard Knight, confirmed there was no evidence of sexual assault. Death was caused by manual strangulation and stab wounds.

There is always a problem in declaring such an attack as motiveless on the basis that the pathologist can locate no sign of a sexual attack. In the case of child strangler John Straffen, whose case is described in chapter 10 of this book, Letitia Fairfield and Eric Fullbrook, who carefully studied his background and the similar kind of pathologists' finding (in that case) that there was no evidence of sexual assault alongside the manual strangulation, comment:

Mrs Helen Fleet. (By kind permission of the Weston & Somerset Mercury)

> It does not follow that, because there is no evidence of interference, the murderer was not impelled by a sexual motive. He might have been alarmed before he could complete his original purpose, or the killing might have been a substitute for the sexual act in some abnormally constituted person. (Fairfield, L. & Fullbrook, E.P., 'John Thomas Straffen 1952' in *Famous Trials 8* edited by James H. Hodge, Penguin 1963, p183)

In a perverse way, the crime that is declared motiveless can therefore be more terrifying to the local population than one with a clear motive of robbery, revenge, sexual attack or a hundred and one other reasons.

In the case of the murder of Helen Fleet, there appeared to be nothing, no real clues, no witnesses hurrying forward and no sign of the small bladed knife used to stab the victim ten times – the wounds extending from under her left arm to the bottom of her abdomen. Such was the local concern about solving this apparently motiveless murder, that a joint venture between the *Weston Mercury* and South Woodspring Crime Prevention Panel set up 'Crime Line', offering a reward of up to £1,000 for information leading to the arrest and charge of the person or persons responsible for the murder of Mrs Fleet. The fact that this horrific murder took place only yards from Worlebury Road and near to the local bus terminus gave hope that somebody had spotted a possible attacker making their escape. Police also reminded the public that Mrs Fleet's car, parked nearby, was a blue Datsun, just in case this triggered an association with someone lurking nearby.

By 3rd April, almost a week later, the police had received approximately 100 telephone calls, a fairly small number for a case of this importance. Meanwhile police search teams dredging local drains did discover a small bladed knife, but its condition showed it had been there for some months. By 10th April the *Weston Mercury* ran a follow-up to its 'Crime Line' initiative of the week before, and reported that six calls to the line had been received and were being investigated.

Already a sense of frustration was implicit both in the style of reporting and the police's disappointment at having no real leads to a murder that must have sent the perpetrator fleeing for cover in a busy area. Then a breakthrough came after descriptions were issued of people the police would like to interview. The first person was described as white, about fifteen to seventeen years old and of skinny build. He was said to have short black hair, a darkish complexion and to be about 5 ft 10 ins tall. He had been wearing a red and grey ski-style jacket. At about 11.30 am on the morning of Saturday 28th March, he had been seen walking toward the water tower in Worlebury Woods, near where Mrs Fleet was discovered. A second man was said to be white, in his early twenties and of medium build. He had what the police said was 'well-styled blonde hair'. He had been wearing a pale green or possibly blue blouson-style jacket, pale denim trousers and grey running trainers. He was actually spotted running along Ashbury Drive at around 12.15 pm. This is a road which leads down from the woods, so it was of great importance to identify the mystery man as soon as possible. The police also included a third person, a young lad around twelve years of age seen whittling wood near to the water tower, but very quickly the lad was identified and eliminated.

By this time the police reported that they had taken nearly 400 statements and had dealt with around 700 lines of inquiry. Nearly 80 officers were assigned to this case. It was looking as if a result could be close by. They decided that it was time to jog even more memories in order to close in on the killer. The following day, Saturday 11th April, they arranged for Bristol PC Jackie Clare to play Helen Fleet in a reconstruction of the fateful woodland walk. Jackie Clare even took Cindy and Bilbow with her to complete the picture. It was also arranged to include the original drive to Worlebury Hill Road. So, dressed in a brown fur coat, woollen hat and brown boots, with the dogs in the back of Mrs Fleet's blue Datsun car, she drove to the exact spot, parked the car at exactly the same time and set off on Helen Fleet's last walk, trying to time herself so as to walk at the same pace as a frail, elderly lady would have managed.

On the Monday immediately following this reconstruction, the police received a call from a woman in a distressed state claiming to know the murderer, but she rang off before giving any details. Naturally police were anxious for her to ring back. By 24th April, the mystery woman mystery caller had rung four times, each time breaking her promise to call by the police station or meet up with detectives. The police believed at this stage that she might be a hoaxer. They were now desperate for a breakthrough, as it somehow seemed inconceivable that they could have collected such good descriptions of suspects, such wide publicity both locally and now nationally, but yet found no one to question with a direct link to the time, place and the incident. A woman on a bus had confirmed a sighting of a youth running from the woods at around 12.50 pm. Police think this is the younger of the two men whose descriptions they had issued: the new witness described him as aged fifteen to eighteen, skinny, with black hair and wearing a red and blue trimmed skiing jacket. This was now a 'before' and 'after' description that matched and was seen as highly significant. At this stage, towards the end of April 1987, the police had interviewed more than 1,100 people and taken 870 statements.

It was a frustrating inquiry, since somewhere close by was a murderer who killed without apparent motive. However, over a month had now passed since the murder of Helen Fleet. Decisions had to be taken. The police decided to release a tape of the mystery female caller. They elicited the support of local radio stations to see if anyone knew her voice or hoping perhaps that the woman, if genuine, would be prompted to call again and this time meet detectives. 'He said he'd done it,' she had told the police, 'some row over the dogs or something got him into a state, perhaps he fell apart. I didn't want to accuse him because he is violent.' That was all she told them.

Five weeks in, 60 officers were still working on the case, having collected 1,200 statements and dealt with around 450 calls to the incident room – but no name, no address to target or specific area or business premises in which to locate a leading suspect. They had visited around 1,400 houses and flats, with lots more still to check, but these were not searches prompted by clues, only by aiming through a process of elimination to cover as much ground as possible. It was a tough job and Detective Superintendent Ray Sarginson was feeling the strain.

The next stage was to issue a photofit picture relating to the descriptions they had so far of the younger man, first seen walking and then running. This graced the front page of the *Weston Mercury* on Friday 8th May, with an accompanying explanation that 'Helen Fleet was seen walking her two dogs near the water tower in the company of this youth'.

Meanwhile, behind the scenes, arrangements were in train to feature this case on BBC TV's *Crimewatch* programme. This would extend the publicity to around 17 million viewers, and it was always possible that holidaymakers, from other parts of the country perhaps, unaware of these events, would see the programme and recall some useful information to help solve this terrible murder. On the programme, which was screened on Thursday 21st May, Superintendent Sarginson told presenter Nick Ross that it was possible someone might be shielding the killer, '... but they should come forward because of the ferocity of the crime'. At this stage around 40 officers were still working on the case but house-to-house inquiries were being scaled down.

After the reconstruction on *Crimewatch* had been broadcast, a call was received. The caller claimed to be the man walking with Helen Fleet, and gave his name, saying that he lived in Weston. He rang off without leaving contact details and to this day has never been traced. Another wicked hoax?

Indeed, now, over 20 years have passed and the brutal, apparently motiveless murder of 66-year-old Helen Fleet on 28th March 1987 has not yet been solved, despite a £7,000 reward having been offered. It is now a cold case waiting for some life to be breathed back into it. It is possible someone reading this very story has that key piece of information to bring a killer (or killers) to justice.

Do you hold that vital clue?

(II) 'IT'S A PUZZLER'

'We haven't even got a motive.'

(Detective Sergeant Les Fowler,
Bath Incident Room, 13th February 1978)

Fifty-two-year-old Beryl Culverwell lived with her husband Anthony, aged 57, at their comfortable detached house, Woodholme, in Widcombe Hill, Bath. Whilst Anthony, a stockbroker, worked in St Nicholas Street, Bristol, Beryl was a busy, well-loved charity worker and trustee, assisting a long-established voluntary organisation called the Bath Maternity Society. Dating from 1886, its goal is to assist young mothers, married and unmarried, who are in financial difficulties. Beryl would visit mothers in hospital or in their home and do whatever she could, giving emotional support and advice and recommending financial help from the Society in appropriate cases – particularly assisting younger married mothers living away from home. She also volunteered at the local community centre in St Marks Road, giving senior citizens a lift back home. Beryl and Anthony were a contented couple who had been married for 25 years. They had two sons and a daughter, all successfully making their own way in life: a happy, close family.

On Friday 13th January 1978, Anthony arrived home from work at 6 pm to a house shrouded in early evening darkness. At first he thought that perhaps Beryl was still about her duties (though she would normally have been back by this time); then he realised that she must be at home, as her Renault car was parked in the drive. Once inside the house, he called her name but there was no answer. Strewn across the kitchen table was some food shopping: bacon, carrots, potatoes and a chicken; and something was burning in the oven – a blackened, burnt pastry. Anthony turned the oven off and now felt very worried. Beryl was definitely not at home – but where was she? There were no messages left for him and it just did not feel right. Occasionally she would visit a young mother within walking distance, and perhaps she had stayed on later than planned, which would be typical of her if the young woman had been upset. Beryl would have stayed and comforted her.

Anthony checked all the rooms and called her name. At last, the only place left was the garage – but why would she be in the garage? Had she had an accident? It is not difficult to imagine the rush of thoughts going through his head. A door led from the utility room directly into the garage, but it was locked from the house side, so it seemed unlikely that she could be there. However, he checked anyway and from that moment his life and that of his children was split apart. His wife was lying in the garage in a large pool of blood. Anthony rushed to her side, calling out her name, but Beryl was completely motionless and blood had been pouring from serious head and body wounds. Nearby lay a kitchen bread knife heavily stained with blood.

Beryl Culverwell.

When the police and ambulance arrived, the inevitable was confirmed – that Beryl Culverwell had been brutally murdered – clubbed viciously across the head and stabbed many times in a frenzied attack with her own kitchen bread knife. The pathologist would later discover 21 separate stab wounds to her body.

129

The most immediate thought was that she must have disturbed an intruder – but if the motive had been robbery, nothing appeared to have been taken. Indeed, she had money on her and her purse was lying on the kitchen table where she had left it after shopping. There was evidence that she had poured herself a glass of ginger wine and was preparing herself some lunch after a shopping trip into Bath, before setting off for a 2 pm appointment with a young mother. She never kept that appointment – the pathologist later estimated that she had died between 1 pm and 2 pm that afternoon.

Further investigation showed that the telephone wires had been cut with secateurs from the garage, which were left lying in the hall, so it seems clear that an intruder did enter the house and was possibly lying in wait or was taken by surprise when she returned home. Puzzling was the fact that there were no signs of a violent struggle in the house. Police thought that perhaps Beryl had fled into the garage to escape the intruder. A more likely guess might be that she had been taken there at knifepoint and once in the garage, for whatever motive, brutally murdered. But why?

Why kill a helpless woman and steal nothing? There was no sexual assault, no obvious motive. There are rare incidents when killing another person is the goal rather than the means to any other deviant act or thieving plan. Was this a highly dangerous psychopath whose only goal had been the murder? Speculation was rife.

BATH WIFE'S GARAGE DEATH RIDDLE

was the *Western Daily Press* headline the following day. The word murder was carefully avoided, as the immediate police classification was that of 'a suspicious death'. The reporter did, however, remind readers that the Culverwells' house was only 300 yards from where widow Winifred Coleman, aged 78, had been found stabbed to death in September 1976. The killer of Mrs Coleman has never been found.

The intensive investigation continued to hunt for clues – it is crucial to discover as much as you can in the immediate aftermath of a crime – before the crime scene and close surrounding area become contaminated and 'tired'. An immediate appeal was put out to local landladies, asking them to inform the police of any sudden arrivals and departures of guests, since the killer might not be from the Bath area. As soon as Monday morning dawned, motorists along Widcombe Hill found their journeys interrupted by a police road block and were then asked whether they had been there on the Friday: if so, had they seen anything suspicious, however vague? Monday also saw the opening and adjourning of the inquest on Beryl Culverwell. The post mortem now officially revealed that she died from loss of blood and shock, the result of multiple stab wounds. It was clear there was a dangerous killer on the loose.

Detectives did discover a bloodstained handkerchief about half a mile from the murder scene on waste ground near Sydney Buildings and were elated at such a tangible clue. These events of course predated DNA analysis but blood matching would have given some indication whether this blood could have been Beryl Culverwell's. Connecting the handkerchief with a suspect would have been more difficult. The discovery of the hand-kerchief led to the theory that the killer might have fled from the back door and across a field, dropping the handkerchief on the way into Bath. His clothes would have been heavily bloodstained and he would not have wanted to leave the house by a public route. An appeal was put out to dry cleaners, asking them to report any bloodstained clothes brought into them since 13th January, and a massive house-to-house inquiry began, with up to 60 officers assigned to the case. Unfortunately, in less than a week, the only tangible clue – the bloodstained handkerchief – had been eliminated. A boy had seen it being thrown away by a man with a nose bleed before the murder could have occurred. Detective Superintendent John Robinson, who was heading up the investigation, said the first week of the inquiry had not gone as well as hoped.

The excitement of a lead began again when several witnesses talked of seeing a yellow Ford Cortina Mark III, not only parked outside Beryl Culverwell's house around 2 pm, but also turning out from the drive of the house into Widcombe Hill at approximately 2.45 pm. Indeed, one witness told the police it contained two men and drove dangerously to the junction, almost hitting another car in its haste. Detectives worked hard and successfully to eliminate from their inquiry a number of cars that had been seen on Widcombe Hill that day, and were left with the mysterious yellow Mark III Cortina – it kept cropping up in witness reports. Are there two killers involved?

Another thought by detectives was whether the killer was the same person who had threatened to kill 84-year-old Minnie Ball in nearby Grosvenor Place, London Road on 22nd December 1977. This man had cut the telephone wires, and took Miss Ball's savings of £62, after having thrown a blanket over her head and threatened to stab her with a knife. Beryl Culverwell's sheepskin coat was lying near to her body: did the killer place this over her head in the same manner as Minnie Ball's attacker?

There were forensic clues found at the original scene that, once analysed, would dramatically change the direction of the inquiry. By 20th January, 400 statements had been taken, but no real leads had emerged until the forensic team pieced together fragments of the broken butt of a double-barrelled shotgun found near to Beryl Culverwell's body.

They now knew that she had been savagely clubbed on the head three or four times with the gun's stock, so heavily that parts of the gun had broken away and been left in the pool of blood around the body. Enough forensic information was gleaned to describe the weapon as a 50-year-old, English-made shotgun, with a Rogers side-lock action, worth between £300 and £500. Attention was now focused on finding the gun. Frogmen searched the nearby Kennet and Avon Canal and local gun-dealers were asked to assist in possibly identifying anyone recently selling, buying or asking about the repair of such a weapon.

From this moment on a whole array of frustrated detection occurs. The inquiry continued by interviewing more than 5,000 staff and students at nearby Bath University but to no avail. Some detectives were now talking of a gang of robbers that might have been responsible, and announced a reward of £1,000 to induce one of the gang to shop the killer. 'There are plenty of clues,' said Superintendent Robinson. 'He must have gone home with bloodstained clothing. He owns a shotgun which is now broken.' A robbery with shotguns at a sub-post office near the Forest of Dean on Monday 30th January was now taken as a serious link to the murder of Beryl Culverwell but no tangible clues existed, only a theory which produced headlines in the *Western Daily Press* such as,

SHOTGUN RAID KILLER LINK: IS THIS THE BATH MURDER GANG?

From lone killer to gang, with only the fragments of a shotgun on which to base the leap, was possibly stretching credibility. Other such raids the year before were now re-examined, and descriptions of two such raiders were issued. By the end of January, with no real progress, the police staged a reconstruction showing a yellow Mark III Cortina parked at the house around 2 pm and then driving away 45 minutes later, hoping that this might jog some memories. When a clear month had passed and detectives took stock, they were faced with the knowledge that, despite 10,000 interviews including door-to-door, road checks and others, the police had no real clues.

Detective Sergeant Les Fowler commented: 'It's a puzzler. We are looking anywhere because we haven't got anything yet, we haven't even got a motive. Robbery was an unlikely motive because nothing was stolen.'

Then, at that very moment came hope. On 13th February a young boy called the incident room to say: 'I have found a shotgun in the hills in Bath. It is all smashed up. If my parents knew, they would tell me to deny it.' He said he did not want the call to be traced and rang off.

Police were desperate for him to ring back or for someone to help trace him. Police also took seriously a vision by a Bridgwater clairvoyant, who claimed never to have been to the area yet described the Culverwells' house and a man running away, throwing something into a nearby canal. He recalled a striking red crew-neck pullover. Police pricked up their ears, as

133

the second-hand gun dealers in the area had also spoken of a man who had tried to sell them a double-barrelled shotgun – he had been wearing a red crew-neck pullover. Superintendent Robinson said, 'In every major inquiry, people who have had dreams or visions come forward and I have found them helpful in the past.'

The hunt for the yellow car, the man in the red crew-neck pullover and the broken shotgun were all positive leads, but not easily chased down unless the public had assisted. On Saturday 18th February, the boy claiming to have found the shotgun called again but rang off without revealing any more details. By this time detectives were getting visibly frustrated, so much so, that when another anonymous caller twice gave significant details over the phone that made police take him seriously, but rang off before arrangements could be made to meet him on an confidential basis, Superintendent Robinson warned the mystery caller saying, 'Come and see us now or we'll come looking for you.'

He never did come and see them; they never did find him, nor the boy, nor the shotgun, nor the yellow Mark III Cortina and, as a result, nor the killer or killers of Beryl Culverwell, who are still sought nearly 30 years on. Television appeals on the BBC's *Crimewatch* programme, and extensive newspaper coverage of the murder, failed to yield any leads whatsoever – it was a dead end and the police were frustrated. The case was gradually scaled down over the years, but of course has never closed. A big push to refresh this cold case was last made in January 2003 when the Avon and Somerset Police launched a public appeal for information. Sergeant Bob Allard said: 'After so many years, we are still really no further forward as to who was responsible. The big question is why was Mrs Culverwell murdered?' (BBC News, Monday 13th January 2003.)

Who and why remains the mystery.

It was Detective Chief Inspector Larry Bill who, whilst confirming the motive dilemma that has beset them all these years, set out a thought-provoking observation:

We feel we have exhausted all lines of inquiry over the years. There is no obvious motive for the murder of

Mrs Culverwell. That is why we would like to hear from anyone who may know something about the murder. It is possible someone may be harbouring a dark secret that they have been living with for the past 25 years, something they want to share with us.

(Newsquest Media Group: 2003)

That dark secret is a little older now – do you know who is keeping it?

Footnote: A lump sum was left from Beryl Culverwell's estate to the Bath Maternity Society. It provides yearly for special equipment to assist the comfort and well-being of a young baby with disabilities assessed by a health visitor as being able to benefit from such assistance. At the time of her tragic murder, friends described Beryl as an 'angel of mercy' to young mothers in trouble. She is still that angel today.

(III) 'A COLD CASE INDEED'

'We were pleased when she came to England because it was a safer country than America – we thought she'd be safer here.'

(Shelley's father Frederick, 18th October 1984)

The 1984 murder of 32-year-old mother of two young children, Shelley Morgan, rates as one of the coldest of all the cold cases that confront the Avon and Somerset team. This unsolved murder should not still be on the open case file after all these years. When a murder case victim is such a very distinctive-looking person, as Shelley was with her waist-length fair hair, large red-framed fashionable glasses, multi-patterned red smock and American accent, out and about in the suburbs of Windmill Hill's Dunkerry Road, she would not pass unnoticed.

Even more to remember her by was the fact she was taking her children Liam (aged ten) and Charlotte (aged eight) to catch the school bus.

If more was needed to trace her movements on this June morning, she was also carrying a very distinctive multi-coloured carpet bag, with a camera tripod visible. She was excited about her plan to go and spend the day taking photographs at Leigh Woods, and hoping to get a good shot of the Clifton Suspension Bridge. Shelley was an artist and would often use her photographs as inspiration for her paintings. Her husband, Nigel Morgan, aged 33, was away staying in a holiday cottage they owned in the Brecon Beacons.

Shelley never returned to meet Liam and Charlotte from school. It was feared that she had had an accident, particularly given the rough and wooded terrain of the area she was planning to visit. Another possibility was that she had had transport problems getting home. Could it even have been one of those rare but documented cases of sudden amnesia – perhaps she did not know who she was any more or where she lived? Or had she planned to leave her family, and had more been packed in the carpet bag than anyone realised? Did she have a secret lover?

All of these questions and many more were posed and considered but at first not much thought was given to the possibility she might have been the victim of a murderous attack. On Monday 11th June 1984 she had set off on a perfect summer morning using a public bus route to Bedminster and then Portishead. However, as the days ticked by with absolutely no sign of Shelley Morgan the grim reality had to be faced that something serious might have happened to her.

Already, by Wednesday 13th June, police working on the accident theory had been using tracker dogs to search the woods, but it is such a vast area that she could have been anywhere. By Thursday, volunteers from the Avon Mountaineering Team were searching the old and dangerous quarries in a section of woodland, but to no avail. Two days before Shelley went missing, 17-year-old Bath schoolgirl Melanie Roads, who lived at home with her parents in St Stephens Close, had been

Shelley had plans that day to get a good photograph of Clifton Suspension Bridge.

discovered stabbed to death in a frenzied knife attack in the Lansdowne Road area*. The attack had happened after she left the Beau Nash Disco Club in the city centre in the early hours of Saturday 9th June. The police had found no clues at the scene of Melanie Roads' murder, and did keep in mind an outside possibility that there might be a connection with the apparent disappearance of Shelley Morgan.

Another possibility that the police considered was that she had been abducted, and that soon a ransom demand would come. Shelley would never have run off and fail to contact her children – that was not in her character. She was cheerful and chatty and loved her family and a home life split between the Bedminster area of Windmill Hill and their holiday cottage in the Brecon Beacons. The puzzle was that, despite her distinctive appearance, unusual accent for the area, and the belief that she had taken the number 359 country bus service in the direction of Portishead, appeals by the police and the media for witnesses on that route to come forward yielded nothing significant at all. An incident room was set up at Nailsea, manned by a team led by Detective Inspector Lew Dark, which received around 25 calls claiming possible sightings. One told the team that a woman matching Shelley Morgan's description had been seen in Weymouth boarding a ferry to the Channel Isles. Another, seen to be significant, was in the Ham Green area on the Portishead road at 11.30 am. Another caller put Shelley further down towards Easton-in-Gordano.

A woman who could have been Shelley Morgan was seen taking photographs from a parapet near the suspension bridge. This and other dead-end calls became routine and tailed off significantly as time wore on. All the police team really had was information about a possible witness, a woman in her 40s with permed ginger hair, wearing a blue jacket, who possibly had spoken with Shelley on the bus and had got off it at Ham Green Hospital. They were also hoping to trace a woman who had been waiting at the bus stop at Ashton Court Lodge between 10.35 am and 10.45 pm on the day Shelley Morgan disappeared.

Towards the end of August Inspector Martyn Shell told the *Bristol Evening Post*, 'We are really no further forward than the day she disappeared. It seems she's joined the 18,000 people who go missing in this country every year.'

Bedminster to the Avon or Portishead area is not very far, around seven miles or so, but it would have involved the missing woman spending long enough on the bus, or waiting for it, to have been noticed by someone. Did she set off in an entirely different direction: south or east of Bedminster perhaps, changing her mind about photographing the Avon Gorge and deciding on a picturesque Somerset village instead?

Shelley Morgan.

In September a very sinister telephone call was received by the police incident room. It claimed that the caller knew where Shelley Morgan could be found and described the location of what they chillingly referred to as her 'watery grave'. The police, of course, took this very seriously, and sent police frogmen to search the spot referred to, but found nothing. They concluded it was a wicked hoax. Other calls trickled into the incident room from time to time, including a claim that Shelley had been seen as a passenger in a yellow lorry. At the same time the Melanie Roads' murder hunt was also making little progress, so the Bath and Bristol police kept in touch in case they should find a connecting clue.

The sheer emotional wrench of Shelley's disappearance, with no real information about what might have happened to her, was taking its toll on her family. Shelley's parents still lived in America (Bloomington, Illinois) and had, of course, been over in England to support their son-in-law and grandchildren. It was difficult to remain optimistic, but to some extent, 'no news was good news'. They knew how serious it was when Shelley missed her son Liam's eleventh birthday in July. They had been holding on to the possibility that she had left of her own accord, and at least would make contact then. When she didn't, they were forced to suspect the worst and began waiting to hear it.

Then, in October, the news came and it was far from good. On Sunday 14th October a boy out playing in woodland near Watercatch Farm in the North Somerset village of Backwell had run screaming to tell of the skeleton he had found in the woods. This proved to be the body of Shelley Morgan, badly decomposed and leaving the bones exposed. She was naked except for torn, maroon tights twisted around her ankles and in brambles nearby were her sandals. There was no sign of her camera, its tripod, her clothes or the carpet bag. Several acres of farmland in the junction of Church Hill Lane and Long Lane, Backwell were cordoned off for intensive forensic examination.

The post-mortem examination at Ham Green Hospital failed to establish a cause of death, and dental records were required to establish positively that the body was indeed that of Shelley Morgan. After painstaking forensic examinations over the next week it was established that Shelley had been sexually assaulted and stabbed seventeen times in the back. It was the most horrific ending to the family's hope that somehow, somewhere she might be alive but perhaps confused or ill.

Her Olympus OM20 camera had been stolen – so at least there was now a possibility of tracing a murderer and bringing justice home to the family – a poor substitute for Shelley but at least offering the possibility of closure. A murder inquiry began in earnest. The new initiative to find the killer of Shelley Morgan followed the same dismal course as the original missing persons inquiry. No real leads emerged at all. Ironically Backwell, where her body had been discovered, was very close to the incident room at Nailsea.

All this time she had been secreted in woodland a few miles east of the police operation. This was totally the wrong direction out of Bedminster and lay south-west instead of her intended north-west journey to the Avon Gorge. Had she been murdered

A reconstruction of the Shelley Morgan case is staged by Crimewatch, *in collaboration with the police.*

at Avon and driven to Backwell? Was Backwell the murder location or had she been dumped there? Where was the murder weapon? A whole raft of new questions was added into the equation.

Inspector Dark said that there were two theories: 'She either got into a car or was forced in before being attacked and left at the scene; alternatively she could have been taken alive to the scene then attacked.' This was never resolved.

By March the following year the incident room at Nailsea was closed down, but Inspector Dark promised, '... the file on her murder will never close'. It was at this time that the influential BBC *Crimewatch* programme agreed with the police to stage a reconstruction of the Shelley Morgan case in an attempt to refresh the public's memory of that June day, and perhaps now direct attention to the tracking of the camera and hopefully a murderer once it had been found. The programme was broadcast on Tuesday 6th November.

Filming the reconstruction was a very difficult but significant day for the family, and particularly for Shelley's parents, who had flown over from the United States to make an appeal to the public on the programme to help catch their daughter's killer. The producer of the programme, Linda Cleeve, recalled how very sad and emotional this day was for the family. Of course there was still hope of catching the brutal killer, but it brought back with a tremendous blow the sheer shocking nature of what had happened to a young mother, wife and daughter. She recalls:

> It was raining very heavily and I drove to Nigel Morgan's house with the kindly police sergeant who'd been with us throughout the filming.
>
> The sergeant said he'd go in the house first to let the family know I was waiting outside. 'They'll obviously find it upsetting,' he said. 'I'll just pave the way and come back and get you.' So I waited in the car, the rain pouring down. I'll never forget it. After about ten minutes, I saw Shelley's husband, this great gentle bear of a man in just his shirt sleeves in the teeming rain holding his two little children by the hand.
>
> He was taking them away so they wouldn't be distressed by me and the film crew coming to talk about their mummy's death. They walked right past the car where I was sitting. I just filled up. I sobbed and sobbed. (Ross, N. & Cook, S. *Crimewatch UK*, Hodder & Stoughton, 1987, pp60–61)

It was a meticulous attempt to replicate Shelley's walk to the bus stop with her two children. They were filming the only part of the journey that was possible to film, setting off from the house to the bus stop. A neighbour of Shelley Morgan broke down in tears when she saw Elayne Sharling, the actress playing Shelley. 'You looked so much like her it was like seeing Shelley's ghost, she confided to Elayne. Linda Cleeve admitted that it was the only time on a *Crimewatch* reconstruction when she felt the distinct presence of another person when no one was there.

'I feel rather stupid saying it,' she said, 'but the actress Elayne and I both felt it at the same time. We'd just finished filming in the house and the crew had left to get ready for some more shots further down the street. Elayne and I were the last to leave and were walking down the hall chatting when suddenly we both felt something. We turned to each other at exactly the same moment and said, "Did you feel that?" I can't explain more but we both felt quite disturbed.' (Ross, N. & Cook, S. *Crimewatch UK*, Hodder & Stoughton, 1987, p60)

Despite the best efforts of the programme and Shelley's father's emotional appeal for help in tracing her killer, the run of bad luck and no clues continued for the police – no substantial leads emerged then and none have done so since. Was Linda and Elayne's experience a missed opportunity? Could it be possible that Shelley was trying to communicate something? Far too fanciful, I suspect, and certainly beyond the realms of investigative possibilities – at least for the police.

The tragic murder of Shelley Morgan is still unsolved. Is it remotely possible that you know something but haven't realised it? Perhaps in 1984 or 1985 you innocently bought a second-hand Olympus OM20 camera, with the serial number 1032853, and lens number 32717520, complete with tripod, and even a distinctive carpet bag from someone in the Bristol or Bath area?

Cold cases may be just that but they are not closed cases because 'there is no deadline for justice'. As Detective Sgt Gary Mason of the Cold Case Team, Avon and Somerset confirms:

'We never forget.'

---

* The brutal stabbing of 17-year-old Bath schoolgirl Melanie Roads also was never solved and remains on the cold case file.

12
CRIMEWATCH TO THE RESCUE

'At approximately 5pm on 18th July 1985, a man in blue overalls was seen outside Roy Page's shop. An hour later the shopkeeper was dead.'

(Ross, N. & Cook, S., *Crimewatch UK*, Hodder & Stoughton, London 1987, p145)

Crimewatch UK was broadcast for the first time in June 1984 and has built and retained an enormous popular appeal. The most common criticism given to it has been based on allegations that the programme's core of real crime reconstructions panders to sensationalism and possibly engenders an unnecessary fear of crime amongst the most vulnerable viewers.

'Don't have nightmares, do sleep well,' became a regular 'catchphrase' of presenter Nick Ross. He told me that he felt he ought to offer some words of comfort at the end of what seemed to be an enormous catalogue of unsolved crimes. 'We thought we were going to raise fear of murder and rape and mayhem,' he said, adding that, 'we got a lot of letters about the nice, reassuring bit at the end.'

However, it is because of these very realistic reconstructions of violent and murderous crimes, showing the real horror, fear and impact on the lives of innocent people, that *Crimewatch* has built up an effective interactive relationship with the public as to 'whodunnit'. Of course, there is still a tension for some between the programme's mission to entertain at the same time that it aims to bring before the viewer extreme examples of the violence and wickedness of real life.

Now, however, there are many instances of how *Crimewatch* has not only speeded up the detection process with its clear visual impact, entering the homes of millions of people, but also in some celebrated cases it has quite possibly saved another victim from fraud, robbery, rape, or even murder.

Indeed, only fourteen months after it began, a meticulously detailed

© David Kidd-Hewitt

Nick Ross.

Crimewatch reconstruction of the 1985 murder of a Bedminster shopkeeper clearly demonstrated the power of a unique interactive relationship between enthusiastic viewers, the broadcast media and the police in effectively tracking down a murderer. Even more to the point, the police were in no doubt that this was a murderer who would have struck again.

———◆———

I t was around 5.45 on Thursday evening, 18th July 1985, when a small group of children began to gather outside a very popular local tobacconist's and, more importantly for them, sweet shop, in the Bristol suburb of Bedminster. 'R. & H. M. Page' was literally a corner shop and a favourite destination for local schoolchildren: a real pocket-money heaven. Roy Page, the owner, was very well liked by all who shopped there. That particular afternoon neighbour Tom Coles, calling to have a chat, was puzzled to find a small gathering of children and a locked shop door. His friend Roy was a diabetic so Tom was worried that he might have been taken ill. He could see a light on at the back of the premises so went home and telephoned the Pages, but there was no answer. Returning to the shop with another near neighbour, they banged and hammered on the door, while the children joined in, shouting through the letter box. The crowd outside grew.

Tom Coles had called Roy's son Brian who, together with Brian's friend Stephen, rushed across to the shop to see what had happened. Stephen climbed over the wall by the back entrance, but soon returned to report that the back door was locked, the curtains were drawn and there was nothing to see. By this time Roy Page's other son Gordon, an electrician, had arrived, also very concerned about his father. Brian spotted a police patrol car and waved it down, explaining why they were worried. Together with Gordon, Brian and Stephen, the police did not hesitate to force the shop doors open, but were choked back by the smell of gas.

Roy Page was unconscious by a cupboard as if he had fallen out of it. It was soon apparent he was dead. Every gas appliance was hissing out its deadly fumes and these were quickly turned off by PC McQuitty. When the ambulance arrived, shortly afterwards, the ambulancemen took over the care of Mr Page.

It was soon established that Roy Page had been the victim of a vicious beating to his head whilst a gag had been forced down into his throat.

His sister Shirley, while visiting the shop earlier, had noticed that Roy had left money lying around, so had collected it up and put it in the safe for him, leaving him alone in the shop at around 4.15 pm. She confirmed that, altogether, around £2,000 had been taken. A major robbery/murder investigation now swung into action.

Detective Superintendent Lew Clark and his deputy, Detective Inspector Bryan Saunders, quickly established an incident room at Broadbury Road police station. They had found two tangible clues at the murder scene. Fingerprints had been discovered on an empty paper bag carrying the name of a chemist's shop, and the killer had dropped a grey ear-piece designed for listening to a portable transistor radio. Although the bag was Roy Page's, the murderer might have touched it in his haste to find something to gag his victim with. From a detection point of view, things were going well. Also, it was quickly established that many people had seen a heavily-built man in the vicinity of the shop wearing headphones and carrying a transistor radio. He had spoken to quite a few witnesses, explaining to them in a strong Welsh accent that he was responsible for detecting gas leaks in the area. Some witnesses described the man as wearing worker's overalls, which supported his explanation.

In particular, the detectives discovered that a man fitting this description had visited other small shops in the suburbs of Bristol, three of them in Horfield that morning, and then around Bedminster on the afternoon of 18th July. All sorts of information was uncovered with the public's assistance. Some witnesses had seen the mystery man hanging around outside Roy Page's shop that afternoon between 4 pm and 5 pm. Others said that he had been seen arguing with Roy Page, also that afternoon. Crucial evidence, however, came from local people whose homes the man had actually visited, explaining he was there to look for gas leaks.

Suffice it to say, no such initiative had been authorised by the local gas board. One home the man visited that afternoon was that of Maureen and Elizabeth Gerrish. They were emphatic that they had no gas leaks but said their near neighbour, Mrs Perkins, had mentioned a smell of gas in her kitchen. As Elizabeth Gerrish had directed him to Mrs Perkins house in Hill Avenue, she had been somewhat embarrassed to see that the man's overall zip had been left open a little too far, and she had noticed that he was wearing white underpants with a blue trim to the waist.

The man called on Mrs Perkins who confirmed to him that she was worried about the smell of gas. However her visitor's foolhardy technique of looking for gas leaks with a lighted match alarmed her. Claiming to have found a leak, it turned out that the man had no tools with which to repair it. At this point he had suddenly become very agitated, started to perspire heavily and appeared short of breath. Gulping down a glass of water from the kindly and concerned lady, he had muttered an excuse and left.

The descriptions and clues were of first-class quality. They now ran from descriptions of the man's appearance, his overalls, his underpants, his accent, jittery manner and the accessories he was carrying – a black box or calculator was also described alongside the transistor radio and headphones. The detectives were confident of finding their prime suspect very soon. Mrs Perkins lived very near 'R. & H.M. Page', and another neighbour, Mrs Jeanette Hemmens, recalled seeing the 'man from the gas board' follow Roy Page into his shop at round 5 pm. It was all tying together very nicely. The final chapter of the suspect's reported movements that afternoon placed him coming out of the side door of the shop at 6.15 pm. This would seem to be rather late and likely to have coincided with the attempts by Roy, Brian and Stephen to find a way in – so it was possible that he literally had just escaped either moments before they arrived or actually whilst they were outside the front of the shop. Indeed, had he been watching the whole time from a distance, as the police broke into the shop with Roy Page's sons?

Unlike the earlier ones, this final description had him wearing glasses, no overalls and carrying a jacket.

Despite a massive photo-fit poster campaign and detailed local and national press coverage, the trail led nowhere. Superintendent Clark commented: 'We knew everything about the man we were looking for, but we just could not find him.'

By August, having built up its confidence with the police and public, and realising what a powerful medium *Crimewatch* had become, its director offered to assist the police in locating their man. The police seized this opportunity with both hands. A reconstruction was prepared and on 29th August 1985 it was broadcast to around 12 million viewers. Roy's sons, Brian and Gordon, had offered a £5,000 reward for any information leading to the arrest and conviction of their father's killer. Ross and Cook comment, 'Seldom in a murder inquiry have so many detectives had so many witnesses and clues and yet got nowhere.' [Ross, N. & Cook, S., *Crimewatch UK*, Hodder &

Stoughton, 1987, p147] Frustratingly, the initial response to the broadcast remained disappointing, but a woman (who had been away at the time the news of the murder had first broken) provided the final confirmation that the man police were seeking had actually been in the shop late that afternoon. When she visited, the shop had been closed and she had looked through the door and seen the man that was by now being referred to as the bogus gasman. According to Ross and Cook's book (p150), 'He looked at her, put his hands together against his cheek, miming sleep and mouthed the words, "He's asleep".'

The witness had then gone home. In retrospect it seems an odd encounter, but she had had no reason to think Roy Page had been murdered by this man. She had shortly after gone away on holiday, so did not know at that time that she had actually seen the murderer at the scene of the crime.

The detectives were in even more despair – the picture of their killer was now stronger than ever, yet for a few days no real leads came into the *Crimewatch Update* programme to suggest a name. However, on 7th September, in the middle of the afternoon, *Crimewatch* viewer Stephen Harfield was driving down Chichester Road in Portsmouth when he spotted a familiar looking man. He was convinced that it was the bogus gasman he had seen on *Crimewatch* the week before. He stopped the car and watched the man hanging around outside a small shop, then went to a telephone and rang the police.

Indeed, the *Crimewatch* factor appears to have worked, given that half a dozen Portsmouth people rang the police to describe seeing the bogus gasman at several locations throughout the area. He appeared to be repeating his Bristol pattern of visiting small shops during the day, preparatory to choosing his early-evening target. A clear description came from Shelia Long, working on her own in a local grocery shop. The customer's heavy Welsh accent, as he purchased a frozen steak pie, was the final confirmation. To her concern he lingered around the doorway before finally leaving. However, these first few calls did not help to catch the man, as he had always moved on by the time the police could get to the scene of a sighting to question him. This was probably more luck than judgement on his part,

The Crimewatch *reconstruction showing the 'gasman' approaching Roy Page's shop.* © Crimewatch UK

as it was unlikely he knew just how familiar a figure he had now become amongst the country's viewing public.

The real vindication of the *Crimewatch* factor came from 29-year-old local man Colin Weaver who, having only seeing part of the *Crimewatch* reconstruction, recognised the man walking along Clarkes Road near the Kingston recreation ground from the photo-fit image.

It was approximately 5.30 pm. Colin Weaver watched him enter the park, sit on the grass and drink some lemonade. He called the police from a nearby call box. When PC Green arrived to check out yet another sighting he realised that the police now had a significant result. A thick-set man in blue overalls was relaxing on a grassy mound – he certainly fitted the description of the prime suspect. The following conversation, recounted by Nick Ross and Sue Cook (see pages 152–153), reveals just how dangerous this man really was.

Constable Green asked the suspect his name. 'Clive Richards', was the answer, in a deep Welsh accent, to which the man added almost immediately, 'Well, Professor Clive Richards, actually.' Asked where he came from, the reply was, 'London, well, Reading, actually.' Asked about his reason for being in Portsmouth, he gave a reply that rang serious alarm bells for PC Green. 'I'm a professor, like I said. I study nonetology and totetology. I am employed by the Department of the Environment. It's a bit hush-hush, actually, but it's to do with conservation. I was in London doing a survey for them into the down-and-outs, that's why I am dressed like this. Good God, you don't think I dress like this normally, do you? I dress like this to blend in.'

Luckily, Clive Richards had no hesitation at all in going to the police station to talk to PC Green a little more about what his 'work' involved. His only concern was not to miss his train back to London: 'I've got to get back as soon as you've sorted out your little problem. I do have people to answer to, you know, being a research director.' It is reported that Constable Green promised to escort him personally to catch his train back, so reassuring the suspect on that point. At Kingston Green police station the priority was to hold Richards until the Bristol detectives could get there. Meanwhile, the contents of his bag provided the final evidence required: a pair of rubber gloves, a heavy iron bar, a sheath knife, some lemonade and, last but not at least, a pair of white underpants with a blue trim to the waist. The metal bar and knife, Richards explained, was his protection from the down-and-outs that he was busy surveying for the government.

PC Green had more than enough evidence to detain Clive Richards whilst an elated Inspector Saunders made haste to Portsmouth. As soon as Bryan Saunders saw the man in custody, he knew that this was the bogus gasman from the *Crimewatch* reconstruction. He recalls:

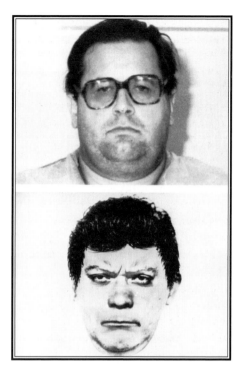

Clive Richards (above) and (below) the photo-fit picture of the suspect.

> I introduced myself, said I was from Bristol, and arrested him for the murder of Roy Page ... he started to sweat profusely and asked for a drink of water. This is the man, I thought, this must be the man, because I remember Mrs Perkins had described the fellow asking for a drink of water. It all slotted in so neatly. It was almost too good to be true.

> (Ross & Cook, pp152/3)

Thirty-five-year-old Clive Richards denied knowledge of the murder of Roy Page and also denied having been in Bristol. He was driven past Roy Page's shop and asked if he had ever visited it, to which he replied, 'No, never.' However, the discarded paper bag found at the scene proved to have Clive Richards' fingerprints on it. He had no grounds to deny anything any more.

The trial was held on 28th April 1986, and by this time it was clear to all those working on the case that Clive Richards was a very dangerous fantasist, a man prepared to murder in cold blood, living in a world of lies. He believed he was a professor of 'nonetology' and 'totetology' who was working in a secret capacity for the Mary Elizabeth Trust. He had convinced his parents back in Port Talbot that he had been offered a post with a Japanese company based in Canada carrying a salary of £52,000. It was a remarkable claim, since Richards was basically an incompetent shopkeeper who had run the family confectionery business and mobile shop into the ground with his ineptitude, and needed money to repay business debts of around £10,000. This job claim had allowed him a brief escape from the family business problems he had caused in order to steal and, as it turned out, murder. He was full of nonsense words for a make-believe world. Indeed, in his own defence, he subjected the court to five hours of gobbledegook mixed with some truths about his life, but denied the murder of Roy Page to the end.

The trial was a long and detailed one, and ended on 7th May 1986. The jury were unanimous that Clive Richards was clearly guilty. Two final comments, one from Mr Justice Rose and the other from Superintendent Clark, show quite clearly the importance we can place on the public identification of Richards that followed *Crimewatch*'s timely reconstruction. Sentencing him to life imprisonment, Mr Justice Rose said: 'You are a clever, arrogant and dangerous man. Had it not been for the observation and prompt action of a number of inhabitants of Portsmouth, I fear you would have committed other very grave offences which you had already planned.' Lew Clark was in no doubt whatsoever that more violence and possibly murder would have occurred in Portsmouth on 7th September, perhaps directed at Shelia Long, working alone in the Spar grocery shop where Richards had bought his frozen pie. Did *Crimewatch* save a life that day?

Think of the way he was armed when he was arrested. He had an iron bar and a dagger. Why did he have that lot? I haven't any doubt myself that he was out to commit robbery at least that day. And, if opposed he would have used as much violence as was necessary to achieve his ends. That's my opinion. That will always be my opinion.

(Ross & Cook, p154)

This was Lew Clark's last case before retirement, the culmination for him of a long career in crime detection and a highly successful outcome to his last assignment. For a certain television programme, it was also clearly the beginning of a new era in discovering 'Whodunnit?'.

BIBLIOGRAPHY

Casswell, J.D. (QC), *A Lance for Liberty*. George Harrap 1961

Fairfield, L. & Fullbrook, E.P., 'John Thomas Straffen 1952' in *Famous Trials 8*, ed Hodge, J.H., Penguin Books 1963

Gaute, J.H.H. & Odell, R., *Murder 'Whatdunit'*. Harrap 1982

Innes, B., *Bodies of Evidence*. Amber Books 2001

Kray, K., *Killers*. John Blake Publishing 2003

Lane, B., *The Encyclopaedia of Forensic Science*. Headline 1992

Ross, N. & Cook, S., *Crimewatch UK*. Hodder & Stoughton 1987

Stratmann, L., *Gloucestershire Murders*. Sutton Publishing 2005

Townsend, P. (webmaster), www.bristolhistory.com

Newspapers:

Bath Weekly Chronicle and Herald.

Bristol Evening Post.

The Times.

Weston Mercury, Somerset and Avon Herald – (all extracts and images so credited are reproduced by kind permission of *Weston & Somerset Mercury* [Archant] South West)

INDEX